GETTING STARTED

GETTING STARTED

The Reading-Writing Workshop
Grades 4–8

Linda Ellis
Jamie Marsh

HEINEMANN
PORTSMOUTH, NH

Heinemann
A division of Reed Elsevier Inc.
361 Hanover Street
Portsmouth, NH 03801–3912
www.heinemann.com

Offices and agents throughout the world

The authors and publisher wish to thank those who have generously given permission to reprint borrowed material:

"Writing Survey" and "Reading Survey" copyright © 2006 by Nancie Atwell. Originally appeared in a different form in *In the Middle* by Nancie Atwell. Copyright © 1998 by Nancie Atwell. Published by Heinemann, a division of Reed Elsevier Inc., Portsmouth, NH. All rights reserved.

Figure 4–2: from "Ten Questions to Ask About a Novel" by Richard Peck from *The ALAN Review*, Spring 1978. Reprinted with permission.

Figure 4–3: from "Dialogue with a Text" by Robert Probst from *The English Journal*, January 1988. Copyright © 1988 by the National Council of Teachers of English. Reprinted with permission.

Library of Congress Cataloging-in-Publication Data
Ellis, Linda.
    Getting started : the reading-writing workshop, grades 4–8 / Linda Ellis and Jamie Marsh.
        p.   cm.
    Includes bibliographical references and index.
    ISBN-13: 978-0-325-00998-8
    ISBN-10: 0-325-00998-8
    1. Language arts (Elementary).   2. Language arts (Middle school).   3. English language—Composition and exercises—Study and teaching (Elementary).
4. English language—Composition and exercises—Study and teaching (Middle school).   I. Marsh, Jamie.   II. Title.

LB1576.E427 2007
372.6—dc22   2007027316

Acquisitions editor: Lois Bridges
Production editor: Sonja S. Chapman
Cover design: Shawn Girsberger
Compositor: Kim Arney
Manufacturing: Steve Bernier

Printed in the United States of America on acid-free paper
11 10 09 08 07   EB   1   2   3   4   5

Contents

Foreword

Where does a person's intellectual life begin? Certainly neither one incident nor one person can take credit for such genesis. We do know, however, that we were present and a part of the intellectual lives of Linda Ellis and Jamie Marsh.

We first met Linda in the summer of 1985 after her second year of teaching. As a participant in a writing institute we conducted at Sam Houston State University in Huntsville, Texas, she was on fire about getting her students to read. By the end of the three weeks, she was on fire about getting her students to write. Concerned about the writing done by her own children, Linda brought boxes of what they had produced to share with the participants. Being an action researcher, she had a box for each child labeled by name, age, and grade. We remember vividly some of Brian's writing—we even included one of his pieces in our book *Acts of Teaching: How to Teach Writing.*

Brian's writing odyssey is revealing. Vibrant and clever books filled his first-grade box. We could still see the tape marks where these stories had hung on Linda's refrigerator. In second grade, Brian wrote more stories, which he published in his self-made books. By third grade, he was going to town, on his way to a rich literate life. But then Linda opened his box from fourth grade. It was nearly empty. Gone were the self-generated stories about Brian's pets and throwing rocks into the creek. Gone were his books with their carefully placed staples down the left side. Instead, a small stack of worksheets covered the bottom of the box. Linda explained, "Fourth-grade testing. The teacher doesn't have time to teach writing; the kids just practice formulas." Fortunately, because of his strong background in reading and writing and Linda's influence, he was able to continue writing.

We remembered Jamie's writing, too. Jamie's boxes weren't much different, so Linda swore that she would intervene with Jamie. And she did. Jamie became Linda's student and, along with her classmates, wrote chapter books in sixth grade. Dana, an honor student, is an avid reader; and we see Jennifer, a first-year teacher, and her students in the pages of this book.

Linda became a certified trainer for the New Jersey Writing Project in Texas, now Abydos Learning International. When we observed Linda in her classroom in a small district in East Texas, the walls were crowded with shelf after shelf of books. Books were everywhere—in baskets, in rotating wire displays, on desks, and in the students' hands. Linda's middle schoolers displayed a passion about their reading and writing that matched Linda's. She had obviously infused them with her love of literacy. Not long after her training, she enrolled in graduate school, and when she asked us about pursuing a doctorate, we did for her what she did for her students—we encouraged.

We have followed Linda throughout her career. She has maintained her status with NJWPT/Abydos Learning—she is now a diamond trainer, with over five successful re-certifications over the past eighteen years. We have been honored to be a part of her professional life, and she honors us in turn.

As a college professor and officer for Texas State Reading Association, she has invited us to participate in conferences and sessions. As a district administrator in English Language Arts, she has shepherded teachers and her daughter to and through the same training she had been through—the NJWPT/Abydos three-week writing institute and its attendant workshops.

And so the cycle continues. We write; we teach. Our student, Linda writes; she teaches. Her daughter, Jamie, writes; she teaches. This cycle brings us to their book, which stands as a symbol for what all teachers are about—we are the vehicles of a grand intellectual process.

It is this cycle, this process, that brings us to write the Foreword.

By synthesizing the work of researchers, educators, and teachers in the fields of reading and writing over the past fifty years, Linda and Jamie provide a book that will serve teachers well in their classrooms. Mother and daughter have grounded this book in the soundness of daily teaching, myriad experiences, and their research.

More, Linda and Jamie have produced a practical guide supported by their combined years in education and their deep dedication to the literate lives of students. We believe *Getting Started: The Reading-Writing Workshop, Grade 4–8* will be part of the intellectual lives of all who read it. Teachers often know what must be done; most only need to be shown a way. Linda and Jamie show teachers a way—therein resides the wisdom of this book.

—Joyce Armstrong Carroll, Ed.D., H.L.D.
and Edward E. Wilson

Introduction

If I have seen further, it is by standing on the shoulders of giants.

— *ISAAC NEWTON*

Enrolled in the final semester of her preservice program, Jamie thought she couldn't possibly be more ready to enter the classroom and *finally teach*. She was fired up, energized, and ready to charge into the teaching profession. Little did she know she was about to fall into a public-school snake pit swarming with outside forces bent on discouraging her vision and persuading her to do a lot of "stuff" during what little time she had with her students.

Luckily, before that happened, she attended a state reading conference and listened to Richard Allington, the keynote speaker. After hearing his presentation, she eagerly got in line to buy his book and have him autograph it. But instead of simply signing his name, he took the time to add a special note: "Jamie, when you get your own classroom, pay attention to the things that really matter."

She understood his message and made a promise to herself that no matter how difficult times got—no matter how much pressure she got from other teachers or administrators to do "stuff" in her classroom or how much pressure she put on herself to do more and more—she would keep focusing on what *really* matters for her students.

Now we pass that advice on to you. We know how difficult it is not to get caught up in the pressure of district curriculum, test preparation, or just simply feeling that you're not doing enough in class. We know what it's like when the teacher next door gets praised for a cute reading or writing activity, one that might be creative and not bad . . . in an ideal world where you have all day to read and write with your students. But we teach in the real world, in real classrooms, where we're *lucky* to have a ninety-minute block (two class periods) a day for language arts and where we often have only half that.

In real classrooms, there is no time to waste on cute activities, on "stuff." There is only time to pay attention to the things that really matter, just as Allington advised Jamie to do. He gave her permission. She continues to give herself permission every time she walks into her classroom. We hope this book will give you permission to do what's right for your students.

Reading-writing workshop, as Atwell called it years ago, or reader's-writer's workshop, as Calkins calls it, or whatever name we choose to give it, provides the best structure for allowing the things that really matter to prevail. We don't get bogged down with the "stuff" that Allington warns teachers about.

And it works—no matter what grade one teaches. Scores go up; low-performing schools become acceptable, acceptable schools become recognized, recognized schools become exemplary. These results are achieved because students are becoming readers who love books, get lost in books, and devour books, and writers who get lost in their own writing.

We believe in kids—all kids. Many years ago banners began emerging in school hallways proclaiming "All Kids Can Learn." We must ask ourselves, is this a mission statement in word only, created because of a mandate, or do we truly believe it? Children continue to enter our schools only to find themselves labeled "at risk," "learning disabled," "dyslexic," or a myriad of similar terms. Children are at risk now more than ever of being held back if they don't pass "the test."

We continue to hear from the nonbelievers: "You are not Nancie Atwell, and this is not Boothbay Harbor, Maine." "I'm just going to wait until the pendulum swings back." "This is the real world and that approach doesn't work here." "We don't have time for the fluff. We have to get ready for the test." "That won't work with *my* kids."

We say right back that workshop is the only thing that *will* work with *all* kids, because it provides the classroom structure necessary to meet the needs of all kids. We have worked with kids in rural school districts, in urban and suburban schools with predominately African American and Hispanic populations, and in small-town schools. We've worked in elementary schools, in intermediate schools, in middle schools, and in high schools. We have watched students (especially struggling readers and writers) in regular classrooms, in bilingual classrooms, in ESL classrooms, and in special education classrooms as their countenances brighten and their eyes light up. In every situation, the kids get better, the scores go up, energy multiplies. Workshop works because it allows us to teach kids, not curriculum. It allows us to let the students lead the way. It allows us to build relationships, to show students we care, to teach based on individual needs.

So why another book? In spite of copious research supporting reading-writing workshop and the numerous books that have been written, we continue to see bland classrooms filled with rows of students all reading the same book or the same story. Teachers continue to hold forth in front of the class. Students continue to write boring five-paragraph essays or to complete worksheets. We continue to encounter teachers who have never heard of reading-writing workshop or who have given up implementing it amid the pressure. Teachers continue to say, "I learned that in college, but I can't do it here," or, "It won't work with these kids." Too many teachers are burning out in our current test-driven environment. Each year there are more benchmarks, more test drills, more curriculums and scope-and-sequences, and more worksheets—an environment that is killing kids and teachers by draining the life out of classrooms and schools.

We want to simplify the teaching of reading and writing by providing ideas for structuring the classroom and getting started until the classroom can take on a life of its own. We have watched so many new teachers struggle. As one principal said at the end of the year, "We gave Susan the structure, told her what to do, and sent her next door to visit a workshop classroom. Ninety-four percent of her kids passed the test. Now this summer she is learning why she is doing what she is doing." Not ideal, certainly. But this is the real world in which many teachers take over a classroom with only a college degree. They face the strenuous and inordinate task of learning while they teach, at the same time making sure all their students pass the test.

Recently a group of preservice teachers volunteered to drive forty-five miles to spend the day in a workshop classroom. They had read *In the Middle*, by Nancie Atwell, and they wanted to see a workshop classroom in action. Seeing was believing: "Wow! It really works!" "I had chills the whole time." "I couldn't believe the energy." "I couldn't believe how much fun the classroom was." "I couldn't believe how happy the teacher and the kids were." "I couldn't believe how fast the day went." "I didn't want to leave. I just wanted to stay." "I wish I had had a classroom like that when I was in school." And this was the classroom of a teacher who had implemented the workshop structure just the year before.

For the past twenty-two years, Linda has implemented workshops in classrooms—for nine years as a middle school language arts teacher in a rural school district and then as a language arts consultant in numerous low-performing inner-city schools with predominantly Hispanic populations, in suburban schools with predominantly black populations, in inner-city special education classrooms, and in ethnically diverse classrooms. Jamie has taught in a fourth-grade suburban school in an economically deprived area, in a sub-urban middle school with a predominantly black population, and in an ethnically mixed sixth-and-seventh grade with many English language learners. It doesn't matter. The techniques we outline here, which are based on learned and observed principles, work because they are real and authentic.

In this book, we want to do for teachers what Carroll and Wilson, Graves, Calkins, Atwell, Smith, the Goodmans, Allington, Hansen, and others did for us early in our teaching careers: convince us that we must teach kids, not curriculum. We want to give teachers the same permission to teach this way. We want to support and encourage other teachers, as those who came before us supported and encouraged us, to create classrooms where students and teachers learn together and where students are given choices and become excited about learning. We want to encourage teachers to create their own workshop classrooms, the kind that students leave behind only in the physical sense, because what they take with them—the power of reading and writing independently—will last them a lifetime.

SECTION I
Reading Workshop

Perhaps workbooks and all skill-and-drill reproducibles should be required to carry a warning: Caution. Sustained use of this product may cause reading/learning difficulties. Conversely books might carry a label that said: Research has demonstrated that regular reading of this product can reduce the risks of acquiring a reading/learning disability.

— RICHARD ALLINGTON

1

What Really
Matters for Readers

So often in our efforts to teach youngsters to respect books and read "correctly," we've taken reading out of children's hands. Reading has become less like romping about in one's own backyard and more like those stifled pained visits to a grandparent's house.

—LUCY CALKINS

Bookcases filled with books of various genres and levels define the boundaries of the classroom library. Book projects displayed around the room showcase students' favorite authors and titles. At the beginning of the period, students may be gathered on the rug for the daily read-aloud. During independent reading, they will be sitting at their desks or lying comfortably on the floor immersed in books of their own choosing while soft music plays in the background. A few students may be in the classroom library or signing up for a conference. The teacher is reading or conferring with a student in a quiet corner. At the end of the period, students—with a partner, in a small group, or gathered on the rug as a whole group—may be discussing the books they are reading.

■ ■ ■

This could be the classroom in which Linda first implemented a reading workshop (then called an independent reading program) over twenty years ago, or it could be Jamie's classroom today. Not much has changed in what we know about reading. The research isn't new. Reading improves through reading. Reading aloud is important. Time spent reading is important. Letting students choose their own books is important. Knowledgeable teachers are important. Talking about books is important. No matter what state, district, or school we teach in, no matter what our students' backgrounds or interests, we must be committed to setting up classrooms in which all students can and will become readers—lifelong readers who get lost in books and devour them. Then and only then will they improve.

What Do Readers Need?

The following principles are not new. They have been proven by years of research as well as classroom experience:

- *Students need lots of time to read.* Reading (like any skill) improves through practice. It makes sense to allow as much time as possible for students to read in school.
- *Students need to read books that interest them.* Students read more when they are interested in what they are reading. If our goal is to improve reading, and reading improves through practice, it makes sense to allow students to select the books they read, because they are encouraged to read more.
- *Students need to be able to read with ease.* If students read books that are easy for them, they'll read more. By reading easy books, students develop fluency and comprehension. They develop a positive attitude about reading. They learn new words in context and from repetition. They will move on to more difficult books if we give them the chance to get comfortable first.
- *Students (in all grades) need to be read to.* They need teachers who read to them. By reading aloud to students, we provide positive models for what good readers do. Listening to their teachers think aloud while reading, students can get engaged in books they may not be able to read alone. They learn what it's like to get lost in a book. Reading becomes fun—something to be savored and enjoyed.
- *Students need to see adults reading.* The teacher needs to be seen as a reader, to find time each period to read silently while the students are reading, usually five to ten minutes at the beginning of independent reading. Our students will take us much more seriously if they see us as readers who share what we are reading with them.
- *Students need teachers who are knowledgeable about reading.* Teachers must understand assessment and how to listen to readers to determine what strategies (if any) they need to be taught. Students need

teachers who know how to get them engaged in texts and keep them engaged. They need teachers who know what's important.

- *Students need access to a wide variety of reading material.* Proximity of books fosters more reading. Students need access to large classroom libraries, but not having one can't be used as an excuse. If teachers believe the above principles, they will find ways to get books for their students. If students are given the opportunity to read, they'll find their own books. Nevertheless, money, when available, should be spent on books, not programs and curriculum materials.

- *Students don't need programs or curriculum guides.* Programs don't teach students. Research has consistently shown that it is the teacher in the classroom who makes the difference (Darling-Hammond 2000). Teachers need to be free from the restraints of curriculum guides and mandated curriculums that attempt to break reading apart into a sequence of skills to be taught and tested. Reading can't be taught that way. The best teachers will find schools and administrators who trust and support them as professionals to set up classrooms in which real teaching and learning can thrive.

- *Students don't need labels.* All students can become better readers. They just need books and knowledgeable teachers who don't label them, who convince them that they can read well, who teach them the strategies they need to get better, and who give them lots of time to read so they can catch up.

- *Students don't need to be grouped by ability.* Students need heterogeneous classrooms led by teachers who know how to take them forward from where they are. In these classrooms all students will improve, and teachers will have more time to confer with those who need the most help.

What Are the Basic Components of Reading Workshop?

As teachers, we must keep our students' needs in mind every day when we walk into our classrooms. Every time we walk into a department or faculty meeting and are told what to do, every time we're questioned by administrators about what we're doing, every time we're pressured to cover the district curriculum and raise test scores, we must stay focused on what our students really need to improve as readers. Everything we plan and do with our students in the limited time we have with them must be important. In real classrooms, there is no time for anything else.

Reading workshop provides the structure that helps teachers keep gimmicks and busy work out of the classroom and concentrate on what really matters for their students. By focusing daily on the basic components of reading workshop, teachers know that all their readers' needs are being met:

- *Reading aloud.* The teacher reads aloud to the students to model fluency and good reading skills and strategies, encourage critical thinking, expose students to different authors and different genres, and share an excitement and love of reading.
- *Independent reading.* The students read silently from books of their own choosing for a block of time. During the first five or ten minutes, the teacher also reads silently from his or her own book. The remainder of the teacher's time is spent conferring with students. The teacher *confers* with individual students to assess and provide individual instruction, focusing on those students who aren't engaging their books.
- *Sharing.* Students share their observations and opinions about what they are reading as a whole class, in small groups, or in pairs. They may also write responses in dialogue journals or response logs and evaluate and assess their own learning and growth as readers.

Figure 1–1 is a typical schedule for reading workshop. To be most effective, this schedule must be implemented daily, and each component is critical. Ideally, one would have a large block of time each day for language arts—ninety minutes, or two forty-five-minute class periods back-to-back. However, if your school permits only one forty-five-minute period a day for language arts instruction, you can still implement a workshop successfully, while attempting to convince administrators that students need more time to read and write every day. (We offer further suggestions for how to organize your time in Chapter 9.)

Whatever the limitations, we all still face the challenge of making sure we are doing what really matters with our students. Everywhere we go teachers

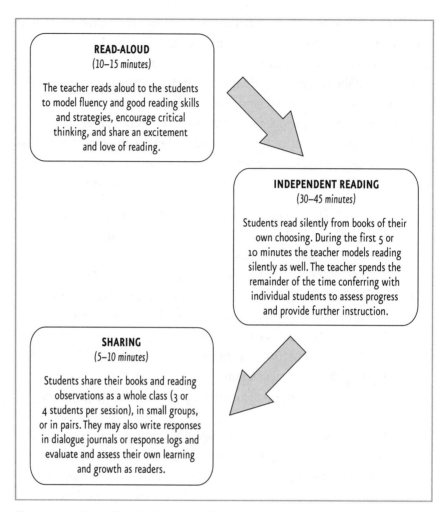

Figure 1–1 A Typical Schedule for Reading Workshop

want and need permission and a tremendous amount of support to withstand the high-stakes-testing pressures. What should be obvious—that reading improves reading—should not be difficult to enforce, as long as the reading is *real*: make sure, every day, that students have books they *can* read, books they *want* to read, have time to read, and have knowledgeable teachers who know how to help them (Allington 2001).

Reading workshop is not a formula. It is not a curriculum. It is not a scope and sequence. It is not a methodology. It is a structure that allows what really matters to happen. It allows students to improve. We encourage you to try—

but not as something students do in their spare time when they've finished the "other stuff," but as how they receive reading instruction, every day.

Some teachers ask, "But won't my students and I get bored doing the same thing all the time?" The answer is no. Even though the structure is the same, what happens within that structure is always different. Whether we read different books aloud to our students or the same favorite books year after year, each class responds differently, and the responses are always refreshing. Because students select books they are excited about, we will always be exposed to new and different books. Lessons are not canned. Responses to the students in individual conferences are not canned. Our teaching is not canned, but rather responds to the needs of individual students. It's an exciting way to teach. So exciting that teachers say (as we did when we began), "But I feel guilty. I feel like I'm not teaching. It's too much fun."

2

Reading Aloud

The single most important activity for building the knowledge required for eventual success in reading is reading aloud to children. . . . It is a practice that should continue throughout the grades.

—The Commission on Reading

The bell sounds, prompting the students in Room 608 to find a spot on the blue carpet near the read-aloud chair, an old rocker I bought at a garage sale and painted bright green.

Some students sit cross-legged. Others grab a pillow and sprawl out on their stomachs or backs. A few students plop down on beanbags or pull up a chair to the edge of the carpet, so as not to block anyone.

Even though each student defines "a comfortable spot" differently, they all have one thing in common—an eagerness to hear what is going to happen next in the book I'm reading to them. Is Rachel going to convince her parents that Julia is a witch? Is Freak going to make it out of this episode alive? Is Luke going to be discovered by the population police? The book lies on the small table beside the chair, spotlighted by a reading lamp. As I sit down, I see questions and curiosity in each student's eyes. Hands pop up. They've been waiting for me. There is rarely a day that I beat them to the carpet.

In the beginning of the year, these new middle school students might be suspicious of this ritual. Are we too old for this? Are we supposed to be acting cool and grown up now? But all it takes to hook them is reading aloud one chapter of a captivating book.

By the end of the year, the overwhelming majority of my students mention in their reflections that this is their favorite part of the class (some even say of the school day). And every day they prove it by scurrying to the carpet, raising their hands with comments—usually more than we have time for—and moaning at the end of each chapter, saying things like, "Ohhhh,noooo! You can't stop there!" "Please keep reading!" "Just one more chapter?" "Can't we just read this book the entire period?" "Let's just stay in here all day!"

These pleas energize me, reminding me how powerful and critical this time is.

■ ■ ■

Figure 2–1

T he best way to begin reading workshop is with a captivating read-aloud. A perfect transition from the noisy hallways, it calms the students down at the beginning of class and sets the tone for what is going to happen during the rest of the period—a lot of reading.

It is our daily opportunity to remind our students that reading is enjoyable, that there are great books out there to read, and that good readers are constantly thinking and predicting and inferring while they read, and it makes them more confident and eager to settle into their own books, applying the same skills and strategies during independent reading.

This time cannot be left out. It is critical, it really matters, and it works!

What Are the Benefits of Reading Aloud?

Many people think that once students learn to read, they don't need to be read to anymore. Wrong. Reading aloud should never end in elementary school. Reading gets more complex as students move up through the grades and the expectations we have of them as readers continues to grow. This is important teaching—modeling what good readers do naturally, then sending students out to read with those models fresh in their minds. It builds the enthusiasm for reading and the skills and strategies needed to become readers who get lost in books.

Reading aloud is a complex activity. It is a critical component of the reading workshop and must happen daily to be most effective. It does not, however, take the place of students reading on their own.

Modeling

When we immerse students in the read-aloud book, we model what good readers do. We model fluency by demonstrating what a good reader sounds like, and we model the thinking processes good readers go through when they read in order to understand and make connections to texts. All reading skills and objectives can be modeled and taught naturally while reading aloud. When good readers read aloud, we're showing students what it's like to be an independent reader.

The questions and discussion before, during, and after a read-aloud allow us and our students to practice and model for one another critical thinking skills such as predicting, inferring, drawing conclusions, visualizing, summarizing, and analyzing story elements (characters, setting, problem, solution, and point of view). We discuss literary elements as they present themselves, and students learn new vocabulary, concepts, topics, ideas, and issues.

Vygotsky (1962) reminded us of what great teachers have done all along: "What a child can do in cooperation today, he can do alone tomorrow." Reading aloud is a perfect opportunity to scaffold and apprentice. Even though we allow wait time and keep our eyes focused on the eyes of the students sitting on the floor around us, we don't get too worried if some students contribute more than others at first. As Frank Smith (1987) also reminds us, "We learn from the company we keep." All students are learning via this process.

Of course, we expect all eyes to be on us while we are reading; that's how we know the students are engaged. We may even move some of them from the back row to the front if we are convinced they are not paying attention. But as students learn that there aren't always "correct" answers, that any answer goes as long as they can support it with evidence from the text, they become more involved. And those who do not join in themselves learn from listening to the conversations of others.

Reading aloud provides an excellent opportunity to model good writing. When Jamie interviewed her students about how they had grown because of read-aloud, most said it had helped them become better writers. They were able to borrow the voices of the authors they were hearing, and they paid attention to what these authors were doing to pull them in and keep them engaged.

Motivating

Reading aloud is also critical in motivating students to want to read, one of the biggest challenges we face in the beginning of the year with students who have not yet discovered the joy of reading. Many students enter the classroom hating reading and not wanting to read, often because they have never been given the opportunity to be successful at it. In earlier grades they may have been forced to read grade-level texts that were too difficult for them and become frustrated. Or they may have read only to answer questions at the end of a story or book for points, a grade, or other extrinsic rewards. Even students who can read may not know what to read or lack the motivation to do so. Reading aloud is our way in, our opportunity to show students how exciting books can be, how much we love reading, and how many good books are out there. Students may first have to get lost in a good read-aloud before they can get lost in their own books.

Building Community

Reading aloud also creates a safe, literate environment and builds a community of readers who love to share a good book or get lost in a story together. And it creates a community of readers who learn to respect the opinions of others. We invite them into what Frank Smith (1985) calls the "literacy club."

As students get lost, together, in the book being read, the characters become their best friends, their enemies, their family members, their pets. They live vicariously through the characters in the book and through each other. There's no better way to build community. They discuss, express differing opinions, argue a little, work through problems together, come to consensus, or not. They learn to value and appreciate differences of opinion. These problem-solving skills carry over to the books they read on their own, to other areas of the curriculum, to mandated tests they may be required to take, and to their relationships with others.

The community that develops also satisfies the desire to belong, a need Maslow (1943) says is a necessity if children are ever going to be ready to learn or become successful members of society. Some people search their entire lives for a place to belong and never find it. If our students don't have a sense of belonging at home and they don't find it at school, they are more likely to search for it in less desirable places—gangs, for instance. We must provide that place to belong by creating a classroom environment in which students can take risks, get lost in the world of books, and become successful, respected members of the literacy club.

Perhaps suggesting that reading aloud each day prevents students from joining gangs is hyperbole. But it is a beginning. Reading aloud is an important component of the workshop classroom because it is a place where students can begin to feel safe, find a sense of belonging, and develop self-esteem.

Introducing Different Genres and Authors

At the beginning of the year we use the read-aloud to introduce students to literature's various genres. Each day we read aloud from a different type—traditional stories, poetry, modern realistic fiction, fantasy (including science fiction), historical fiction, biography, and informational books (Figure 2–2). By immediately sharing a book (or portion of a book) from each of these genres, we not only expose students to the different types of books but also entice them to branch out and read them.

Some students feel a certain pride when they realize they like a particular genre. It makes them feel special. As Kendra said, "I love modern realistic fiction. I feel like I'm experiencing the lives of the characters." Or as Alex countered, "Well, I like historical fiction because I can travel back in time." Students may form their own clubs within the classroom as they gravitate to classmates who are reading the same genre.

Many older struggling readers or students who haven't yet become readers are not ready to jump into chapter books. Nevertheless, they grab an overly difficult chapter book for independent reading. They've gotten the idea that they must read chapter books because they've outgrown "baby" picture books. Beginning the year by reading picture story books aloud removes that stigma, let's them know it's okay to read these books. Even the best readers like them. Seeing that prominent members of the literacy club enjoy reading easy books makes it okay for them to read one, too.

Some teachers, who have collected books in each genre and stored them in labeled baskets in the classroom library, like to follow up a genre read-aloud by giving students time to explore a few books in that genre. This is

- *Traditional:* Books or stories that began as oral tellings and have been passed down from generation to generation. They have a predictable structure since their original purpose was to teach morals. The characters are flat; typically, the message is if you are good, good things will happen; if you are bad, bad things will happen. This genre includes folktales, fables, myths, legends, and epics.
- *Fantasy:* Stories that have some element of make-believe—animals talking, witches, and so on.
- *Science fiction:* A form of fantasy that expands on some element of scientific evidence, examples may include visits from outer space, visits to other worlds, cloning.
- *Poetry:* Condensed, artistic writing with a certain rhythm (and sometimes rhyme) that relies heavily on imagery, sound, meaning, and an emotional connection with the reader.
- *Modern realistic fiction or contemporary realistic fiction:* Fiction set in modern times, characters are dealing with issues and problems that contemporary children might encounter.
- *Historical fiction:* Stories set at least twenty-five years in the past, with characters caught up in the problems and events of that time period.
- *Informational:* Nonfiction books that teach about a specific subject (books that teach concepts, like counting or the alphabet, are included in this genre).
- *Biography:* Informational nonfiction about a real person's life (includes autobiography).

We have been truly inspired by Teri Lesesne through classes and workshops we've taken with her because of her vast and always current knowledge of children's literature. Other resources for learning about genres include Barbara Kiefer, et al.'s *Charlotte Huck's Children's Literature in the Elementary School* (2007) and Donna and Saundra Norton's *Through the Eyes of a Child: An Introduction to Children's Literature* (2007).

Figure 2–2 Genre Definitions

especially helpful if the school library doesn't open until the second or third week of school, which is often the case.

A caution here for those who alternate days between reading workshop and writing workshop: If you begin with genre introductions, have reading workshop every day until you have introduced all the genres. Otherwise, the introductions will take too long. You don't want two or more weeks to pass before you allow students to read their own books or before you begin reading a chapter book aloud.

What Are Some Good Books to Read Aloud?

Students typically like books that have characters about the same age as themselves who are dealing with some of the same life issues. Although we make a point of reading various genres throughout the year, starting off with a good fiction book (particularly a mystery) hooks readers every time and demonstrates to them just how exciting books can be.

Most important, we must be sold on any book we choose. Students can sense whether we are engaged in the book we're reading aloud. Because our attitude toward reading is contagious, our excitement and love of reading must be evident. When pressured by school and district curriculum requirements to read particular class novels, we must always keep our goal as a reading teacher foremost in mind: "Why am I doing this? To help students become better readers and lifelong readers." They will improve as readers only if they have opportunities to practice it successfully. They will practice most when they enjoy reading. This is why reading aloud is critical: we are modeling that good readers love reading and get lost in books. So if your school or district requires your students to read a particular novel, then feign interest and use it as a read aloud until you can convince them that not all students need to read the same novel at the same time.

The following are just a few read-alouds suitable for readers in grades 4 through 8, old favorites as well as more current books:

- *Holes*, by Louis Sachar
- *Bud, Not Buddy*, by Christopher Paul Curtis
- *The Watsons Go to Birmingham*, by Christopher Paul Curtis
- *When Zachary Beaver Came to Town*, by Kimberly Willis Holt
- *Trino's Choice*, by Diane Gonzales Bertrand
- *Joey Pigza Swallowed the Key*, by Jack Gantos
- *No More Dead Dogs*, by Gordon Korman
- *Because of Winn-Dixie*, by Kate DiCamillo
- *The Tiger Rising*, by Kate DiCamillo
- *Maniac McGee*, by Jerry Spinelli
- *Freak the Mighty*, by Rodman Philbrick
- The Harry Potter series, by J. K. Rowling
- *A Series of Unfortunate Events*, by Lemony Snicket
- Betty Ren Wright mysteries
- *Killing Mr. Griffin*, by Lois Duncan
- *Summer of Fear*, by Lois Duncan
- *The Other Side of Dark*, by Joan Lowery Nixon
- *Whispers from the Dead*, by Joan Lowery Nixon
- Any Joan Lowery Nixon or Lois Duncan mystery for adolescents

We also choose books from the following resources. Since these lists change from year to year, consult the websites for the current choices:

- ◼ International Reading Association's "Choices" book lists, selected by children and young adult readers from around the nation, available online at www.reading.org/resources/tools/choices.html.
  - Children's Choices are published in the *Reading Teacher* each October.
  - Young Adults' Choices are published in the *Journal of Adult and Adolescent Literacy* each November.
- ◼ State-recommended reading lists. State library associations have recommended reading lists and information about state awards.
  - Texas awards the Texas Bluebonnet for grades 3 through 6, the Lone Star for grades 6 through 8, and the Tayshas for high school. See www.txla.org/html/reading.html.
  - California awards the California Young Reader Medal in five categories based on grade levels and age. See www.california youngreadermedal.org.
- ◼ The American Library Association–Young Adult Library Services Association book lists and awards. See www.ala.org/ala/yalsa/ booklistsawards/booklistsbook.htm.
- ◼ The American Library Association's Newbery Medal and Honor Books. See www.ala.org.

How Do I Get Students Engaged?

Perhaps some students in the classroom have never read a book (or never read a chapter book). Gathering everyone for a daily read-aloud gives them an opportunity to get lost in a book and become part of a community of readers. We insist that all eyes are on us. This is not a time to go to the rest room, pass out papers, sharpen pencils, or attend to any other duty. It is a time to listen.

Predicting
We always begin by asking, "What do you think this book will be about?" We remind students to use the title and illustrations on the cover to help them

make predictions. Predicting makes them want to find out whether they're right. It builds interest.

Then we read the first chapter, asking questions and thinking aloud as we go, as good readers do when they are reading. This can't be canned; it has to stem from our own immersion in the story. Trying to teach skills in an artificial way kills a good read-aloud. When we finish the first chapter, we ask students to predict what will happen next. The first chapter always takes a little longer, but if we do a good job of getting the students involved at the outset, they're more likely to stay involved through the remainder of the book.

Charting Story Elements

After reading the first chapter, we chart the elements all stories have in common—characters, setting, problem, and solution. We ask when and where the story takes place (setting) and what the problem appears to be at this point, prompting students to look below the surface. For example, in Lois Duncan's *Summer of Fear*, the obvious problem is that Rachel's aunt and uncle were killed in a car wreck. However, digging deeper, we might predict that their orphan daughter Julia's coming to live with Rachel's family and sharing Rachel's life and her room (and maybe even her boyfriend) may make Rachel jealous.

Charting Characters

Next we list each character on the board (or projected transparency or chart paper)—as many as twelve characters may be introduced in the first chapter—to show how books can get complex very quickly (a major difference between children's books and young adult books). Then we analyze the characters as a class: "What was Rachel like?" "She had red hair." We write *red hair* and connect the phrase to Rachel with a line. Gradually students begin to make inferences: "She is responsible because she was left in charge of the house." "She is caring because she brought her mom and dad coffee and offered to go with them." "She is mature because most teenagers don't act like that." If the students just name a characteristic like "responsible," but don't tell why, we ask, "Why do you think that? What in the book makes you think that?"

Someone might also mention a character flaw: "She is jealous." "Why do you think so?" "Because she's worried about sharing her home and family with a new sister." We might go back and reread the appropriate section of the text: "'Crazy,' I echoed with a faint stirring of uneasiness. What would it be like to share my home and my family with a ready-made sister whom I didn't even know?" We then discuss the importance of authors' demonstrating weaknesses as well as strengths to make the character more realistic and believable.

By the time we finish a thorough reading and discussion of the first chapter, students are hooked and want to read more. We don't feel guilty if this takes most of the class period. If the students are engaged and interested, it is time well spent. We are investing in a captivating read-aloud that will continue for the next several weeks.

How Do I Keep Students Engaged?

Each day, at the beginning of the period, the students gather on the rug to listen to the next chapter. We expect engagement, we demand engagement, and we get it.

Summarizing and Predicting

Each period we begin by asking students to summarize: "What happened in the last chapter?" "What did we find out yesterday in the story?" We follow with: "What do you think will happen today?" "Why do you think so?" We teach them that good predictions are logical, based on evidence from the text.

Character Analysis

Then we read one more chapter, stopping at appropriate points to allow students to predict or discuss a character's actions, motives, and so on. We tell students how characters are revealed and developed by what they say to others, how they treat others, what others say to them, how others treat them, what they do, and what they think. We bring out examples as we read. (In third-person narratives, characters can also be developed by what the narrator reveals about them.) This helps students not only understand the characters in the story but also develop the characters in their own writing. It also teaches them to think critically, to infer and draw conclusions; for example, Rachel is caring because she brought her parents coffee and she offered to go with them.

Point of View

We also discuss the point of view of the book and the advantages and disadvantages of first person and third person. With first person, for example, we may be able to get more involved in the story because we live it vicariously through the narrator. We see what she sees, hear what she hears, think what she thinks, taste what she tastes, and so forth. With third person we can see into the thoughts and actions of all the characters, so we learn more, but we may not get as involved with any one character, which may limit our ability to get as lost in the story.

Foreshadowing and Flashbacks

When reading young adult books, we also teach foreshadowing and flashbacks, which don't typically occur in children's books. We discuss these as they occur in the story. It's easy for inexperienced readers to get confused by a flashback.

Comparison/Contrast

Students particularly enjoy books that have been made into a movie. In our classrooms, we show the movie after reading the book aloud and allow the students to compare and contrast the two versions. They typically find the book to be better and are quite surprised and disappointed that characters and scenes have been altered or left out altogether. We discuss the reasons, the most important being that movies last approximately two hours and it takes much longer to read a book. Other reasons can be arbitrary; for example, students may be quite disturbed to find that in the movie *Summer of Fear*, the dog, Trickle, is a horse because the actress who plays Rachel, Linda Blair, likes horses. This changes the story considerably, and students are not happy about the change.

A major goal of reading aloud is that students will learn to visualize the scenes in the book. When one of our students first saw Julia in the movie *Summer of Fear*, he exclaimed loudly, "She looked better in the book!" Helping students make these connections between books and movies can be a powerful motivation to read the books on which movies are based.

What's the End Result?

By the time we've finished reading the book, we have modeled all the reading skills found on any test, but in the context of real reading, not as isolated skills taught one at a time. When good readers read, they use all these skills repeatedly. Trying to teach them in isolation is artificial. Read-alouds encourage students to think more critically about what they are reading while they are reading. We think aloud with them as we read, modeling how a good reader's mind works. We then send them off to read independently with this model in mind and their brains primed to use these good reading strategies and skills on their own.

Reading aloud also gives us an opportunity to hook students on certain authors or to expose them to different genres. Whenever we read aloud, many students want to read other books by that author. Listeners couldn't help but get involved in a good Lois Duncan or Joan Lowery Nixon mystery. So we bring in all our Lois Duncan books or all our Joan Lowery Nixon books, and students rush to check them out, snatching them up like candy.

Our students continue to confirm for us what research has consistently shown, that the degree to which a child has been read to is the greatest predictor of that student's eventual reading success (Anderson et al. 1985). The influence of reading aloud on struggling readers' attitudes toward reading and their eventual improvements in reading and on the overall success of all readers as they conquer ever more complex books cannot be underestimated. Neither can its ability to build community and set the stage for independent reading. It is our invitation into the literacy club.

3

Independent Reading

> [V]ery little of our theory can be attributed to instruction. Only a small part of what we know is actually taught to us. . . . We learn to read by reading, by conducting experiments as we go along.
>
> —FRANK SMITH

"Find a quiet, comfortable spot for reading."

So saying, I signal the beginning of independent reading. As much as the students would love the read-aloud to continue, they have learned that this next part of our workshop is also essential to helping them become better readers. Just as basketball players need to practice playing basketball every day in order to improve, so readers need to practice reading every day. Independent reading is their time to practice.

I watch the students move quietly to their reading spots. A few stay where they are, while others choose more secluded areas of the classroom: curled up in a corner, tucked into a nook between bookshelves, sprawled underneath a desk. Some students even choose to sit at their desks or tables. It is their privilege to choose the spot where they are most comfortable and least distracted, as long as they are reading the entire time.

I turn on some soft music, grab my own book, and choose a spot to read for the first five or ten minutes, a spot where I can see all my students and make sure everyone is on task. My reading with them not only minimizes distractions and movement, allowing students to get immersed in their books more quickly, but also lets me model that I too am a reader who continues to practice and improve. My students love to see me doing what I ask them to do. I read until everyone is settled and has had time to get back into their books, picking up where they left off. Then it is time to teach again—to confer with individual readers.

■ ■ ■

Figure 3–1

Why Does Independent Reading Really Matter?

Whether we call it IR (independent reading), SSR (sustained silent reading), DEAR (drop everything and read), FCR (free-choice reading), FVR (free voluntary reading), or MSSR (monitored self-selected reading), a block of time must be given to students every day to read independently from books of their own choosing. Daily reading practice helps students gradually tackle more complex material. Reading books they can and want to read fosters further reading. The more they read, the better they get.

When reading independently, students may read wherever and whatever they want as long as they read. Only by getting lost in books, taking an unconscious delight in what they are reading, do they learn to think critically and comprehend. This higher-level thinking will improve their reading skills and assist them in doing better on any standardized or state-mandated, criterion-referenced test. It can be the turning point to their becoming lifelong readers.

When students move into more complex material containing foreshadowing, flashbacks, and more (and more complex) characters, they need models and they need time. Research has consistently confirmed that reading improves through practice (Goodman 1987; Smith 1985; Anderson et al. 1985; Allington 1994, 2001, 2002; Krashen 2004b. Most intermediate and middle school readers and second-language learners have the skills and strategies they need to improve in reading; they just need time to practice. If we want our students to improve, they must have this time. Even the best readers need it, and struggling readers need even more of it to catch up.

Research has demonstrated that students who read more score higher on norm-referenced achievement tests. A seminal study published in *Reading Research Quarterly* (Anderson, Wilson, and Fielding 1988, p. 292) examined students' reading scores and the time they spent reading outside school. The findings showed a positive correlation between the amount of independent reading and reading achievement:

Variation in Amount of Independent Reading

Percentile Rank	Minutes / Day (Books, Magazines, Newspapers)	Words / Year
98	67.3	4,733,000
90	33.4	2,357,000
70	16.9	1,168,000
50	9.2	601,000
30	4.3	251,000
10	1.0	51,000
2	0.0	8,000

Our own experience verifies that the avid readers in our classrooms have the highest scores on any achievement test. But most of our students have plenty to distract them out in the world and won't read on their own unless we allow time for it in school. Some teachers say, "Well, they can do that reading at home. When they are in school, I have to teach." But why? If time spent reading is what improves reading, doesn't it make sense to do this in school? Yes, we will still teach, but that teaching will look much different.

What Does the Teacher Do During Independent Reading?

As stated earlier, we spend the first five or ten minutes reading, too. Students take reading much more seriously and settle down faster with their own books when their teacher is part of the reading community. This also allows us to share what we're reading with our students.

We spend the remainder of the time conferring with individual students. Teaching one-on-one is the only way to meet the needs of every child in a highly diverse classroom. We retreat to a quiet corner of the classroom and have students come to us instead of going to them, because the quiet atmosphere in the classroom must be preserved. Students sign up for a conference when they finish a book, if they want to change books, or if they have a question about what they are reading. (The sign-up board can be a corner of the chalkboard, a dry-erase board, or a laminated chart hanging in the classroom.) Or we may instigate a conference ourselves if a student is obviously not reading.

Students sometimes get so excited about getting to spend time one-on-one that teachers can become overwhelmed by the volume; suspending conferences for a short while may help students get immersed in their books again. Although students are expected to have enough reading material to last the allotted time, they may occasionally need to go to the classroom library to check out a new book. Some teachers suspend this privilege if students abuse it. Other teachers preempt the problem by allowing books to be checked out only before or after school. The individual teacher determines the severity or laxity of these kinds of policies. Preserving the serenity of the environment is the goal.

We typically don't start having conferences until about the second week of school so that students can first concentrate solely on reading. When conferences are added to the schedule, the students whose names are on the conference board come to our table one by one. (If we are just "checking in," we may visit students in their reading spots.) Some students need more conferences than others, and conferences in which we teach reading strategies take precedence. When the conference is over, the student draws a line through his or her name and taps the next person on the list lightly on the shoulder to signal the next turn. This way, those waiting for a conference don't have to keep looking up.

Figure 3–2

Conferences allow us to get to know individual students' strengths and weaknesses as readers, their interests and attitudes toward reading, and their specific taste in books. They are a time to assess, teach, provide feedback, and build relationships. The old adage, "a child doesn't care how much we know until he knows how much we care," holds true.

How Do I Help Students Choose Appropriate Books?

A book is appropriate when the student is interested in it and can read it with ease. We first remind students that it is important to choose books that interest them. Why? Because they'll read more. And what happens when they read more? They become better readers.

Too often students aren't able to choose the books they read, especially in the content areas; however, even in those classrooms it makes sense that they should have a degree of choice within the particular topic or theme. Reading and writing should, of course, be integrated across the curriculum. But in reading workshop students *must* be able to choose what they want to read voluntarily, not as an assignment. The goal of the reading teacher is to improve reading and to build lifelong reading habits.

Students must also choose books they can read with ease. To that end, we teach them the five-finger rule in the beginning of the year:

> When you pick up a book, turn to any page. Begin reading. Turn down a finger for every word you don't know. If you reach five fingers on one page, the book is probably too difficult for now. It doesn't mean you won't be reading that book later, but for now you need something you can read with ease.

It's a simple rule to learn and follow, and it gives students permission to read easy books. We assure them that reading improves through reading lots of easy books and that they'll be able to read harder books by the end of the year. We tell them, "If there are too many words you don't know, and you can't figure them out from the context, you're likely to abandon the book." We tell them they can improve two or more grade levels in a year if they just read. The main requirement is that they have a book or books that will last the entire thirty minutes of independent reading (or whatever time is allotted—the more the better).

Some teachers wonder, "But can I let my sixth graders read *Junie B. Jones* or *Captain Underpants*? Those books are so easy. They're never going to be ready for the test." We say, "They're never going to be ready for the test if they aren't allowed time to devour those books." Students won't be bored. When they outgrow those books, they'll know it. They'll move on. If they aren't bored, they aren't ready to move on. Even students who have high test scores, if they aren't readers yet, must have opportunities to read books they're interested in no matter the level. We model through our read-alouds, we nudge, we encourage, but ultimately it's the students' decision. As long as they are engaged in their reading, we know they are getting better.

Unfortunately, even some librarians don't understand the reading process. A librarian told Linda that he wasn't going to order easy books for the intermediate school library because "these students are in fifth and sixth grade and they need to be reading fifth- and sixth-grade books." She cringed. This was on a low-performing campus where only 56 percent of the fifth graders had passed the state reading exam the previous year. Some were fortunate enough to be in classrooms in which they were able to read easy books purchased by teachers with their own money. Other students—most, in fact—were not so fortunate. But the librarian stood firm. Another lesson, for another book— librarians need to be familiar with reading theory.

How Do I Know Whether a Student Is Really Reading?

You'll know whether your students are really reading. Our eyes and ears are our greatest assessment tool (*kidwatching,* to use the term coined by Yetta Goodman [1978]). As we scan the classroom during independent reading, our own book in hand, our eyes pick out those who aren't engaged in their books—they flip through the pages, their eyes move from something in the room to the page and back again, or they stay on the same page.

If a student isn't engaged, we call her or him to the conference corner or perhaps hold a brief conference in place, whispering so as not to disturb the serene environment:

- "How do you like your book?"
- "Read a little for me." If the book is too difficult, we reteach the five-finger rule and convince the student that he will be able to read the book later.
- "What do you like to do in your spare time?" or "If you weren't in school today, what would you be doing?" By tapping into the student's interests, we can guide her to a book of interest. There's nothing more powerful than going immediately to the shelf, removing a book, and saying, "Try this one. I think you are going to like it," or showing up at school the next day with a book just for that student. Your efforts will show the students you know who they are and care about them, and that book may be the one that hooks them on reading.
- "Do you want to change books or keep this book?" If a student insists on keeping the book, we say, "Then I must see you reading. You have a choice of what book you read, but you don't have a choice of whether you read. When you are in this class, you must read. So it's important that you have something you are interested in and that you can read with ease."

Then the student goes back to reading while we move on to our next conference, always checking to see whether our pep talk has been effective; if it hasn't, the student may need some of the strategy lessons described in the next section.

The conference is a critical teaching venue, the place where we identify the individual and varied needs of our students. Many students will not need us.

We always keep focused on our goal: creating lifelong readers who get immersed in books and who will read long after they leave our classroom.

If students are reading, we leave them alone. As Richard Allington adamantly told a group of conference participants years ago, "Quit bothering the kids!" He said that teachers get really uncomfortable if kids are "just" reading or writing. We don't have to constantly "teach" for our students to learn. Their reading will improve if we just let them read. Our task as teachers, as Lucy Calkins (1987) reminds us, is to put ourselves out of a job.

How Do I Help a Reader Who Is Struggling with Text?

Students who are not getting involved in the text are likely to be struggling readers. The most powerful teaching in the classroom (along with reading aloud) happens when knowledgeable teachers assess individual readers' strengths and weaknesses and help them develop effective reading strategies. If a student is not engaged, we have to find out why. It may be that the student hasn't yet experienced the deep places reading a good book can take us. But it may also be that the student doesn't have the necessary strategies. Here's what to do:

- First, determine whether the book is appropriate. Have the student read a page and apply the five-finger rule. If the book is too difficult, help him find an easier book. The text needs to be something the reader can read with at least 90 percent accuracy with assistance and 95 percent accuracy on his own.
- Second, listen to the reader read. What does he do when he doesn't have someone there to help? What strategies is he using? What strategies is he not using? Do a miscue analysis (see Appendix E).
- Third, ask the reader to retell as much as he remembers about the story. When he has told you everything he can, prompt him with questions like these:
  - Are there any (other) characters in the story?
  - Where does the story take place?
  - When does the story take place?
  - Is there a problem in the story?
  - Is there a solution to the problem?

The Reading Miscue Inventory (RMI) came about as a result of Kenneth Goodman's research, beginning in the 1960s. Goodman saw reading as a process in which three types of information (graphophonic, syntactic, and semantic) are integrated through the processes of sampling, predicting, confirming, and correcting, the primary aim being to comprehend meaning. Goodman's theory of reading challenged the predominant theories of his time that focused on accuracy. In his theory "errors" (negative) became "miscues" (positive)—by-products and mirrors of the reading process—because if readers are to be successful, they must be actively involved in the reconstruction of a message. The reading task, according to Goodman, is not to get all the words right, but to get *meaning* from the text. Goodman taught us that if a reader's aim is to make sense of the text—to get meaning—reading becomes easier. His research with real readers in real texts, not in laboratories, found that good readers are using all three cueing systems simultaneously and struggling readers are not (Goodman 1973).

Our understanding of the cueing systems (see Figure 3–3) helped us understand the reading process, and this understanding has since informed

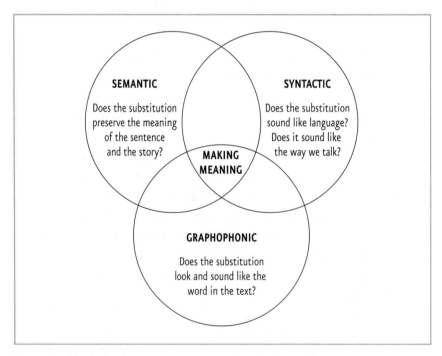

Figure 3–3 The Cueing Systems

how we listen to and assist readers. Finding time to do a formal miscue analysis for every reader in the classroom who struggles is difficult, but over time you will automatically listen to readers in this way.

There is too much emphasis in schools on speed and accuracy without examining the quality of the reader's miscues or determining what a reader is doing in the allotted time. It's not the number of miscues that students make that matters; all readers miscue. It's not the speed with which they read; some readers are faster than others. Many times readers slow down when they begin to improve because they are rereading, self-correcting, and stopping to ask themselves questions in an attempt to make sense of the text (comprehend meaning). Without really listening to what the reader is doing and why, speed and the number of miscues tell us nothing.

Instructions for conducting a modified miscue analysis are included in Appendix E. A thorough analysis of a student's reading provides valuable information for working with struggling readers and for conferring with parents, administrators, and other teachers. The process will also teach you how to listen to a student and let the assessment guide future instruction.

How Do I Use Assessments to Inform Instruction?

There are a number of ways to gain information about your readers. Here are some examples and their purposes.

The Personal Interest Inventory (Appendix C) has two functions:

1. It helps us get to know the student and begin building a trusting relationship.
2. It reveals the student's interests and enables us to help her select books and writing topics.

The Burke Reading Interview Modified for Older Readers (Appendix D) identifies the reader's schema for reading. In other words, it tells us what the reader thinks he does when he reads (which may not be what he actually does). Most struggling readers overuse the graphophonic cueing system. When we ask the first question on the Burke Reading Interview, "When you are reading and you come to something that gives you trouble, what do you do?" the struggling reader will usually answer, "Sound it out," or "Ask someone." Readers who overuse the graphophonic cueing system to the exclusion of semantics and syntax will not improve. Readers who rely on someone to tell them the words they don't know will not get better. Readers need more tools.

A miscue analysis reveals students' reading patterns—their strengths and weaknesses. In every case, if a student is struggling with text, she is not using all three cueing systems, typically overusing graphophonics (even though she may not be using it effectively) and underusing semantics and syntactics. Our goal, of course, is to assist the struggling reader in using all three cueing systems simultaneously. We offer strategies for doing just that. These strategies may be used in individual classroom conferences or as tutorials outside the classroom. Students must be able to read with at least 90 percent accuracy, with help, in the context of books of their own choosing.

How Do I Help Students Who Can't Read?

The following strategies (Gillet and Temple 1986) have proven effective in helping the most severe struggling readers or students who can't read:

- *Echo reading.* Read a sentence or two aloud. Have the student immediately repeat what you read while looking at, and, if necessary, pointing to the words. Read only one or two sentences at a time, or even one long phrase, to allow the student to use his short-term memory as he echos what you have read.
- *Choral reading.* Read aloud in unison with the student. This procedure is more difficult than echo reading and is best used with easy material or with text that has been silently previewed or echo read with the student. Choral reading, with your voice leading and providing the model, is an excellent way for the struggling reader to practice oral reading without the anxiety of going solo.
- *Assisted reading.* Begin by echo reading from easy text that the student has chosen. Gradually begin leaving out some of the words you think the student knows, having him fill in the omitted words (the cloze procedure). As the student begins to take on more of the reading, teach him contextual and structural analysis strategies for figuring out the words he may not know or has trouble recognizing. As the reader becomes more confident, he will begin to pick up more of the text. Praise him often.

What If the Student Can Read but Struggles with Text?

Contextual analysis and *structural analysis* work together for older struggling readers and must be a starting point for students who can read but struggle with text (Gillet and Temple 1986). The *cloze procedure* combines these two strategies. The text should be on an independent reading level (95 percent accuracy) or instructional reading level (90 percent accuracy).

Contextual analysis has proven most successful with struggling readers who aren't using context to help them with words they don't know. These readers fixate on a word and won't move past it, trying to sound it out letter by letter. Using decoding attempts alone interrupts the flow of ideas and slows comprehension. It is difficult, if not impossible, to identify and comprehend a word and the meaning it contributes to a sentence when it is considered in isolation. We need to teach these readers to quickly call a word that makes sense in context and keep going. To teach children to use the semantic cueing system for meaning, ask them to try and use the story to make sense of the word:

- "What would make sense there?"
- "If you were telling me this story, what would you say here?"
- "What is a word that would make sense there?"
- "Thinking about the story as it's happened so far, skip the word and read to the end of the sentence, then come back to that word and think, *what are some words that would make sense there?*"
- "Make it make sense."

Every child who has been immersed in the English language knows its structure. He wouldn't say "I the store to went my mom with," but rather, "I went to the store with my mom." Expecting text to follow a predictable pattern helps them when they read. For example, if a child reads, "I went to the pretty [instead of party]," her sense of language structure alerts her that something is amiss.

To teach students to use the syntactic cueing system for structure, ask:

- "Does that sound right?"
- "Does it sound like language (the way we talk)?"
- "Can you make it sound like language (the way we talk)?"

Second language learners especially have trouble here because the structures in many languages are unlike that of English. Immersion through reading aloud, independent reading, and conversations is critical.

Through *structural analysis* students can also be shown how to break down polysyllabic words into parts:

- Teach them to cover up parts of the word to highlight recognizable units (*de bate able, un like ly*).

- Ask, "What parts do you know?"

- Say the parts together as you uncover each part, blend them together, and put them back into the context of the sentence.

This strategy, like all other strategies, must be done within the context of real reading activities.

The *cloze procedure* helps the reader use context to form hypotheses about unknown words, thus encouraging risk taking. The reader inserts words that make sense and support the author's message. Doing this requires thinking along with the author, using prior information, and following the semantic (meaning) and syntactic (structural) clues provided by the words surrounding the blanks. It makes the reader more sensitive to contextual clues and better able to use them efficiently when reading. Here's how it works:

- Copy a page from the text the student is reading.

- Cover every fifth, sixth, or seventh word.

- Let the student guess what the words are, teaching her that the eye is always moving ahead.

- Ask, "What are some words that would fit?" "What are some words that would fit that begin with [whatever letter is appropriate]?"

Help students realize that it isn't important to know all the words when they read. Tell them that readers learn new words all the time by using contextual clues. Over time, by hearing or seeing the same word in print in various contexts, we learn new words. We can comprehend meaning if we know 95 percent of the words, and the meaning of what we read is the most important thing, much more important than knowing every single word.

How Do I Help Students Develop Fluency?

Poor word recognition and slow, word-by-word reading reduce comprehension. The following strategies help students develop reading fluency:

- *Model fluent reading.* Teacher modeling is crucial to developing fluency. This takes place during the daily read-aloud, but it can also happen in individual conferences. Too often, poor readers are grouped with those of similar ability and, therefore, hear only other disfluent readers reading aloud. Instead, read aloud the first hundred words or so of a book the student chooses. Echo reading and choral reading (described earlier) are other important opportunities to model fluent reading.

- *Provide time for independent reading.* Reading, like any skill, improves through practice. Students must read daily from books on an appropriate level.

- *Ask students to write.* Students should write daily on topics of their own choosing. Writing not only improves writing, it also improves reading.

How Do I Help Students Who Struggle with Comprehension? What if a Student Can Read but Won't?

Some students can call words perfectly, but they don't remember anything they read. Obviously, these readers are not engaged in the text. The following strategies improve comprehension and get students engaged and keep them engaged in text:

- *Directed Listening-Thinking Activity (DLTA).* This strategy, developed by Russell Stauffer (1980), is modeled by reading aloud to the entire class, but it must also be modeled in individual conferences with struggling readers.

  - Choose a book you know the student will be interested in (typically, the book she has selected for independent reading).

- Before reading the book aloud, have the student predict what the book will be about.
- As you read, continue to have her make predictions about upcoming story events and then compare her predictions and assertions to what the text says. Model higher-level thinking by predicting, drawing conclusions, analyzing characters, discussing point of view, using context to figure out words and learn new vocabulary, and so on. (These strategies were modeled in Chapter 2.)

Reading aloud provides a model for what good readers do, and comprehension comes first. Students need to participate in a lot of listening/thinking activities. As they become better listeners, they will become better readers and learn vocabulary. Having heard a word before makes it much easier for students to read the word when they come across it in print.

■ *Directed Reading-Thinking Activity (DRTA).* This strategy, developed by Stauffer (1975), is like DLTA, except the student reads to the teacher in an individual conference. Begin with a prereading activity in which you ask open-ended questions (requiring prediction and hypothesis) that can be answered in many ways and that will encourage divergent thinking. The reader will then have set his own purpose for reading: discovering whether his predictions were correct.

- Read the first chapter or the first few pages of a book with the student.
- Ask her to predict what will happen next: "What do you think will happen? Why do you think so?"
- Ask her to read a predetermined amount (a paragraph, a page, five pages, a chapter—whatever you think she can handle). Tell her, "When you have finished reading, raise your hand. I'm going to come back, and I want you to tell me everything you can remember about what you just read." (Students typically eagerly raise their hands and tell you what they remember.)
- Assign another predetermined amount of reading.
- Continue this back-and-forth dialogue.

This strategy holds students accountable and causes them to focus on meaning as they read because they know they will be retelling. This improves comprehension of and interest in fiction and nonfiction and develops critical reading and thinking.

■ *ReQuest procedure.* This activity makes reading fun and fosters critical reading and reading for meaning (Manzo 1969):

- You and the student both read a prescribed passage silently (one paragraph, several paragraphs, or a page—however much you think the student can handle).
- The student asks you a question. If you cannot answer the question, you may look at the passage to find the answer.
- You both read another prescribed passage, and you ask the student a question.
- Continue alternating questions.

Students love this strategy because they take on the role of the teacher, and you have an opportunity to model higher-level questioning techniques. For example, the student may ask, "What color was Mary's dress?" You may ask, "Why do you think the dress was red? Was there significance to the color?" You're teaching the student to have a conversation about the story instead of an interrogation.

■ *Guided practice.* This strategy focuses readers on thinking and making meaning as they read (and students love it):

- Ask the reader to read for five minutes from the book he has chosen.
- At the end of five minutes, have him turn the book over and tell you what he remembers.
- When he finishes, ask him to look at the passage and add or subtract details.

While the student reads, you can be off to another conference, then return when the time is up. Retelling immediately helps students feel successful, builds stamina, and teaches them to think as they read.

How Do I Combine These Strategies in the Classroom?

In every case, if a student is struggling with text we begin with contextual analysis and structural analysis strategies. When students are taught these two strategies, they flourish. Echo reading, choral reading, and assisted reading are sometimes used if needed. DLTA is always used when we read aloud to the class each day. Next come comprehension strategies like DRTA, ReQuest, and guided practice.

Any strategy, of course, must be followed with lots of time to practice. Readers need to discover a desire to read, and reading should be fun. Good readers become risk takers by not worrying about each word they don't know. They concentrate on comprehending meaning rather than calling words. Become interested in what the students read, and encourage them to talk about what they are reading to you and to each other. Urge them to go to the public library and the school library to check out books.

When students know that reading *must* make sense, reading becomes easier. When they know that language has a certain structure, reading becomes easier. When they don't get overwhelmed by long, polysyllabic words, reading becomes easier. Matching letters and sounds is the least effective tool (cueing system) if used alone. When readers use their knowledge that reading must make sense (semantics) and that what they are reading must sound like language (syntax), they don't have to rely so heavily on the graphophonic cueing system.

As readers move up through the grades, particularly when they hit third and fourth grade, they can become overwhelmed with multiple-syllable (polysyllabic) words and words with Greek, Latin, and other language influences. If they have been taught to rely too heavily on the graphophonic cueing system (phonics) and aren't using the semantic and syntactic cueing systems effectively, reading becomes more challenging. To repeat: successful readers use all three cueing systems simultaneously when they read.

The most important principle to remember is that the brain of the successful reader is always attempting to make sense of the text. We don't look at every letter and every sound in every word. The following passage (source unknown) demonstrates how our brain and our eyes work together to create meaning from very little as we read:

Aoccdrnig to rscheearch at an Elingsh uinerntisy, it deons't mttaer in what order the ltteers in a word are, the only iprmoetnt thing is that the frist and lsat ltteer are in the rghit pclae. The rset can be a total mses and you can still raed it wouthit a porbelm. This is bcuseae we do not raed ervey lteter by it sief but the word as a wlohe and the biran fguiers it out aynawy!

Teaching students only to "sound out words" hobbles them. It's like telling doctors they must prescribe penicillin for all their patients. Instead, doctors perform a variety of assessments, and the analysis of the test results determines the prescription. We as reading teachers must be as knowledgeable. We must assess each student to determine what strategy or combination of strategies that student needs. Diagnosis and instruction are ongoing processes.

By finding appropriate-level texts, by choosing books according to interest, by learning strategies as they are needed, and by being in an environment where reading is promoted, students will begin to improve, and they will begin to notice their own improvement. But they *must* have time to practice. Most students who can read well enough to learn a few strategies get caught up in easy books, practice, and improve.

What Are Some Favorite Books of Readers in Grades 4 through 8?

Students in Linda's classroom twenty years ago were reading R. L. Stine's Fear Street series. Students in classrooms today are reading R. L. Stine's Goosebumps series. Students twenty years ago were reading Lois Duncan, Joan Lowery Nixon, Betty Ren Wright, and Barbara Cooney. Students today are still reading books by those authors. Harry Potter, Captain Underpants, and Junie B. Jones didn't exist twenty years ago. Some authors come and go. Some books come and go. And some hang around for an incredibly long time.

Inventories
The best way to find out students' favorite books is to ask them. A reading inventory we give students at the beginning of the year (Appendix B) asks them what they like to read and who their favorite authors are. Some students respond with a long list, others admit that they've never finished a book. We also have them fill out a personal interest inventory (Appendix C). This helps us get to know the students so we can help them find books they will love.

Book Talks/Teacher Recommendations
Reading is contagious. If we are excited about books, our students will get excited about books. Students listen to our recommendations. We give book

talks (on various genres and subjects) all year, especially at the beginning. We take trips to the school library and have the librarian talk about his or her favorite books and list the books most frequently checked out by other students. We frequently visit our favorite Internet websites (ala.org, txla.org, and reading.org), libraries, and bookstores to stay up-to-date on award-winning, nominated, and recommended books. We have special baskets, shelves, and displays in our classroom libraries, highlighting popular books.

Book Clubs

Book clubs (Scholastic has several popular ones; you can sign up to receive their monthly catalogues by visiting www.scholastic.com) are a great way to excite students about books. Book clubs allow teachers and students to purchase books at a fraction of their cost in bookstores. They also allow teachers to earn bonus points, which can be used to build classroom libraries. Book clubs stimulate interest in books and energize the classroom, especially when the new books arrive; students can't wait to get their hands on them.

Peer Recommendations

Students listen to the recommendations of their peers. At the beginning of the school year, we post recommendation charts and favorite book lists, created by the previous years' students, in the classroom library. It doesn't take long before our new students are creating their own charts and lists to post, not only in the classroom but around the entire school (Figure 3–4). And as students get excited about reading in reading workshop, they naturally share what they are reading with others.

A Final Word

A baseball coach watches his players from the sidelines. A swimming coach watches her swimmers from the edge of the pool. When they see the players or swimmers in action, they know what to teach next. The same is true for reading teachers. Instruction must be individualized and based on the needs of each student. No preset program can improve reading. It takes the eyes and ears of a knowledgeable reading teacher to understand the reading process and know what strategies good readers use. Only the knowledgeable reading

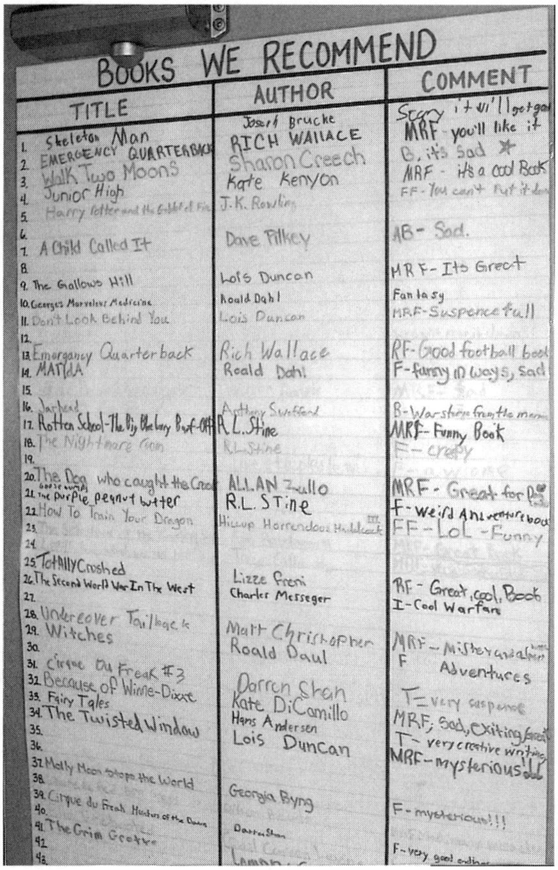

Figure 3–4

teacher, who listens for, identifies, and praises the reader for those strengths, and who identifies the reader's weaknesses can begin to teach the reader the strategies he is lacking. The knowledgeable reading teacher engages her students and keeps them reading books they can and want to read. The knowledgeable reading teacher understands the power of reading aloud. She knows how necessary daily reading time is.

4

Sharing Reading

> Rather than asking students to deal with texts in prescribed ways, we would like to see students responding to texts in terms of how they, both as readers and as persons, are different as a result of having read them.
>
> —SUSAN HYNDS

I finish conferring with a student about the book he is reading and check the clock. Ten minutes left. I walk toward the middle of the room, whispering, "Find a stopping place."

Slowly, breaths and sighs become audible around the classroom as students mentally emerge from the world of their books and physically emerge from reading nooks. A few students wail, "But I'm at a really good part"; others plead, "Just a few more minutes." Glancing at their watches or at the clock on the wall, they are amazed time has flown so quickly. "That couldn't have been thirty minutes."

I revel in these few moments of transition, thrilling as I watch engaged readers reluctantly come back to the realities of the classroom. Oftentimes, many of them have forgotten where they are. They have been lost in a place where real time doesn't exist. I know what this feels like.

As the students put away their reading folders and I announce today's groupings, I hear several students already telling each other what just happened in their books.

■ ■ ■

Why Does Sharing Really Matter?

Sharing is natural. Students are social—especially middle school students. Given the opportunity, they would spend all period sharing everything that is going on in their lives and the lives of everyone else they know. They want to

Figure 4–1

talk to one another, and we want them to share what they are reading, so why not give them a special time to talk about their books in class? Sharing is the perfect way to end the period. Sharing books fosters reading more books and improves overall classroom participation. When students know they will be sharing, they are motivated to pay attention to what they are reading. Sharing is another opportunity to assess students' comprehension of and interest in what they read.

We try to set aside the last five or ten minutes of reading workshop for sharing, but as the school day's demands increase in the higher grades, formal sharing may not be possible every day. While not ideal, this is okay. Students will share their books with one another naturally when they are excited by what they are reading.

How Can I Group Students for Sharing?

Some days we are able to have a *whole-group share*. This is especially important at the beginning of the year because it allows us to model what sharing is all about. As students talk about the books they are reading and recommend their favorite books, we acknowledge and validate their various choices and opinions, affirming that it's okay to enjoy reading. Whole-group shares at the beginning of the year help create a community of readers who like to share what they're reading with one another, thus increasing their motivation to read.

Obviously, not every student will have a chance to speak during a whole-group share; four or five students are about the most that can be accommodated in ten minutes. Also, since the entire class is listening, we never force students to share; we ask for volunteers. As students get used to sharing and become more familiar and comfortable with one another, they become more comfortable sharing aloud. And as we get to know the students better, we may nudge those who are reluctant to join in. For instance, if a student has told us in a conference how much he enjoyed a book, we might ask him if he would be willing to share the book with his classmates, since his recommendation might give other students an idea for what to read next.

Sometimes we set up *small-group shares*, either at tables or on the floor. And sometimes students *pair share*, turning to a nearby student to discuss their books. In this case we might say, "Today we are going to pair share. Find a partner near your reading spot to share with for a few minutes."

Small-group and pair shares are especially useful on days when the read-aloud or independent reading takes longer, and only a few minutes remain. More students get an opportunity to share.

How Should Students Share?

Students can discuss what they are reading in many ways, and in a reading workshop the choice is usually theirs. But there are days when it's beneficial to guide their discussions, have them focus on something particular about their books.

Informal Shares
Informal shares are free and open discussions. We model them for the whole class at the beginning of the year, then allow students to have these conversa-

tions in smaller, more comfortable settings as the year progresses. These discussions are typically spontaneous and unplanned and depend on the books students are reading, how much they are enjoying them, and where they are in them.

Students who are really caught up in their books often can't wait to talk about them, while students who are not as keen on theirs would rather listen. Regardless of who shares, allowing readers to have these discussions not only generates ideas about what they might want to read next (or instead) but also emphasizes that reading can and should be enjoyable and that books exist that offer this enjoyment.

On informal share days, we make a general statement like, "Share the book you're reading with your group," perhaps reminding students that they can discuss whatever they want: what's happening in the book, with themselves as readers, how they feel about reading, and so on. We might explain that spontaneous discussions that occur naturally are authentic and meaningful.

Strategy Shares

Sometimes, however, a read-aloud may spark a particular conversation or minilesson that we want to emphasize. For example, if a read-aloud generated a lot of predictions and a discussion about how good readers predict, we might ask groups to use that particular strategy during sharing time: "Today in your share groups, I'd like you to continue making predictions about the books you're reading independently. Share a prediction of what you think will happen next in your book and why you think that. Remember, good readers make logical predictions based on evidence from the text." Sharing like this gives students another opportunity to practice skills or strategies that were modeled, taught, and practiced during the read-aloud.

Focused Shares

There are also times when we want students to focus on a certain question or questions that will help them make connections to other texts, to the world in which they live, or to events in their own lives or the lives of people they know. In that case, we present a guiding question (see Figures 4–2 and 4–3) for students to respond to, whether in writing or in a share group. (We might write the question on the board, project it on a transparency, or hand it out on a piece of paper.)

1. What would this story be like if the main character were of the opposite sex?
2. Why is the story set where it is (not *what* is the setting)?
3. If you were to film this story and could not use all the characters, which characters would you eliminate and why?
4. Would you film this story in black and white or in color?
5. How is the main character different from you?
6. Why or why not would this story make a good TV series?
7. What's one thing in this story that's happened to you?
8. Reread the first paragraph of Chapter 1. What's in it that makes you read on?
9. If you had to design a new cover for this book, what would it look like?
10. What does the title tell you about the book? Does it tell the truth?

Adapted from Peck (1978).

Figure 4–2 Ten Questions to Ask About a Novel (Peck 1978)

First reaction	What is your first reaction or response to the text? Describe or explain it briefly.
Feelings	What feelings did the text awaken in you? What emotions did you feel as you read the text?
Perceptions	What did you see happening in the text? Paraphrase it—retell the major events briefly.
Visual images	What image was called to mind by the text? Describe it briefly.
Associations	What memory does the text call to mind—of people, places, events, sights, smells, or even of something more ambiguous, perhaps feelings or attitudes?
Thoughts, ideas	What idea or thought was suggested by the text? Explain it briefly.
Selection of textual elements	Upon what, in the text, did you focus most intently as you read—what word, phrase, image, idea?
Judgments of importance	What is the most important word in the text? What is the most important phrase in the text? What is the most important aspect of the text?
Identification of problems	What is the most difficult word in the text? What is there in the text or in your reading that you have the most trouble understanding?
Author	What sort of person do you imagine the author of this text to be?
Patterns of response	How did you respond to the text—emotionally or intellectually? Did you feel involved with the text, or distant from it?

Figure 4–3 Dialogue with a Text (Probst 1988)

Other readings	How did your reading of the text differ from that of your discussion partner (or the others in your group)? In what ways were your readings similar?
Evolution of your reading	How did your understanding of the text or your feelings about it change as you talked?
Evaluations	Do you think the text is a good one? Why or why not?
Literary associations	Does this text call to mind any other literary work (poem, play, film, story—any genre)? If it does, what is the work and what is the connection you see between the two?
Writing	If you were to be asked to write about your reading of this text, upon what would you focus? Would you write about some association or memory, some aspect of the text itself, about the author, or about some other matter?
Other readers	What did you observe about your discussion partner (or the others in your group) as the talk progressed?

Figure 4–3 *Continued*

Why Book Projects?

Recommendations and book talks are two ways for students to share their favorite books with one another. A *book project* is more elaborate, and very different from a typical, old-fashioned book report. Sharing a great book in a creative way is much more enjoyable than preparing a perfunctory summary. Remember, we want to create a community of readers who share their excitement about books and reading with one another.

At the end of a grading period or quarter, we have students choose their favorite of the books they've read and come up with a novel way to present it to the rest of the class. A list of book project options is included in Appendix F. Students will find plenty of ideas to showcase their individual strengths and interests, but needn't be limited to these suggestions. Inspire them to let their imaginations soar! Some students may decide to read the same book so they can do their project together. That's fine, too.

The presentation days become reading celebrations, and the projects are left on display until the next series of presentations. Projects typically get more sophisticated as the year progresses and students learn from one another. (If you videotape the presentations, parents at open houses can see how much

Figure 4-4

reading is happening in the classroom and how eager students are to share their favorite books. And having this wider audience prompts students to work even harder on their projects.)

What About Written Responses?

Sometimes teachers like to have students respond in writing to what they are reading. (Some states include a written response to literature as part of their standards.) Here are two possible methods of written response.

Dialogue Journals

We first learned about *dialogue journals* from Nancie Atwell (1987). Some teachers use them to have their students write to them, a peer, or a parent every week; then the person written to writes back. This is a good option, as long as the entries are not graded and students enjoy this form of communication. However, if it becomes a chore and students have to be nagged and coaxed to keep the journal going, it loses its power and effectiveness. Remember, the purpose of any assignment is to motivate more reading, to create lifelong readers. Ask yourself, would I want to stop reading in order to write to someone about what I just read if I were really absorbed in a book? Does this motivate us to read more? Considering how little time we spend with students each day, we need to concentrate on what really matters.

Hexagonal Writing

Hexagonal writing teaches students to respond to a single piece of literature from a number of perspectives.

We learned Hexagonal Writing from Joyce Armstrong Carroll and Edward Wilson (1993). We like the technique because it teaches students to respond to a single piece of literature from a number of different perspectives.

- *Literal level/plot summary.* Tell the story in your own words.
- *Personal allusions.* Does this story make you think of something or someone in your life?
- *Theme.* What is the author trying to tell you?
- *Analysis/literary devices.* Choose a scene and discuss the figurative language used, giving examples.
- *Literary allusion.* How is this story like other stories you have heard?
- *Evaluation.* Did you like the story or not? What in the story made you think or feel that way? What in the story did you especially like or not like?

Hexagonal writing may be used to examine books the students have chosen themselves, books you have read aloud, or even poems. Some teachers ask students to jot down insights, questions, or thoughts in their response logs or on sticky notes while they are reading so they can refer to them later.

A Final Word

We promote critical thinking if we set up environments in which our students have conversations about books, not interrogations. Nancie Atwell (1987, 1998) says these discussions should be like those that take place at the dining room table. Richard Allington often poses the hypothetical example of someone asking literal-level questions of friends as they are coming out of a movie theater: "What color dress was Gwyneth Paltrow wearing?" That's not the real world. In the real world of reading books and seeing movies and sharing them with our friends, we have genuine conversations: "What did you think?" "How did you like it?" "How about that scene where. . . ."

We must always evaluate why we do what we do as teachers. There must be a purpose for sharing—it shouldn't be contrived—and that purpose must always involve promoting more reading and more enjoyment of reading. We want to create lifelong readers who continue to read when they leave our classrooms, not students who dread coming to class because they haven't completed the reading log, or who hate to read because they know an activity or an interrogation or a report awaits them when they finish.

SECTION II
Writing Workshop

Writing is most important not as etiquette, not even as a tool, but as a contribution to the development of a person, no matter what that person's background and talents.

— DONALD GRAVES

5

What Really Matters for Writers

It is important to remember that what children do as writers depends largely on the context in which they write and on their backgrounds as writers. This is why scope and sequence charts on writing are inadequate and perhaps harmful. Furthermore, even within any one writer, development does not consist of forward-moving progress. One day the writing is good, one day it is lousy, and often what seem at first to be regressions turn out to be the moments of imbalance through which new levels are reached.

—LUCY CALKINS

Student writing covers the walls and is shelved next to books by their favorite authors. In our classroom, students become authors themselves, publishing their work by adding it to the classroom library for others to check out and read. Various types of paper and writing utensils are arrayed on countertops, readily available for student authors to use, and a colorful board is filled with student name cards tacked underneath labels indicating the different stages of the writing process. Pieces of chart paper summarizing our ongoing minilessons dangle from a clothesline stretched from one end of the classroom to the other, reminders of the various writing techniques we've discussed.

At the beginning of the period, students gather on the rug in the meeting area for a writing minilesson. Afterward, they grab their writing notebooks and search out a perfect writing spot for the day. Some students remain in the meeting area, perhaps lying down on the rug. Some go in search of nooks and crannies that offer more privacy. Some move back to their desks or tables or curl up underneath them.

Regardless of where they choose to write, students know they are to choose spots where they can immerse themselves in writing on topics of their choice. Spots where they are the least distracted. Spots where they can concentrate on their writing and remain on task for the duration of independent writing. We have discussed the importance of good writing spots, and I monitor their choices closely at the beginning of the year.

Soft music begins playing in the background. As they begin to write, I, too, grab my writing notebook and write.

Before I know it, it's time to put my writing notebook away and begin conferring with individual students. Students understand that it's now okay for them to move to a quiet corner for their own peer conferences.

At the end of the period, my students are immersed in their writing, and I am reluctant to interrupt; I want to let them go on until the bell rings. But I remind myself that it is also important for these writers to have a few minutes at the end of class in which to give and receive feedback. It is our time to share ideas, topics, praise, advice, thoughts, questions, and so on. It is our time to build relationships, to better understand one another as writers and as individuals. It is our time to say, "Good job!" and "I like how you did that!" and "Oh, that has happened to me!" and "What a cool idea!" Sharing their writing brings my middle school students together at an age where social pressures work toward separating them into rigidly defined groups and categories.

And so I whisper once again, "Find a stopping place and come join me on the floor." Reluctantly at first, one by one, they find a spot in our share circle. As the circle grows I see their attitude begin to shift: Oh yeah, I want to keep writing, but this is when I get to show off my work and receive compliments. This is our time to pat ourselves, and one another, on the back.

■ ■ ■

As reading workshop is to readers, writing workshop is to writers; reading and writing go hand in hand, working with and for each other. When students are writing, they are engaged in purposeful reading, creating words on the page and learning how to revise these words to improve clarity and style. Writing is just as important to improving reading as reading is.

Students must have uninterrupted blocks of time each day to write; writing improves through practice. Gradually, independent writing will take up most of writing workshop, the minilesson being just a brief reminder. Students gradually take ownership of their own writing and of the environment and structure of the classroom as they internalize the techniques and strategies learned from the minilessons we present and the authors they are reading. Our job is to put ourselves out of a job (Calkins et al. 1987).

What happens in the beginning of writing workshop sets the tone for the rest of the year. It's critical to establish our expectations: organization, structure, and commitment. Students need the safety and predictability this provides. We expect that they will follow the rules, and we are firm about the consequences if they don't. We also expect that they will write. Students know and understand that they have a choice of what they write, but they do not have a choice of whether they write. We expect that when we say write, they will write.

Chapter 6 contains several prewriting activities that will generate enough topics to get students off to a successful start. They will eventually drift away from personal narrative to other genres like poetry and various types of fiction or nonfiction, but we begin with personal narrative because students can more easily write about experiences they have lived. It is easier to teach them to extend real experiences.

Once the workshop takes on a life of its own, students will be at different places in the writing process during independent writing—they will not all be doing the same thing at the same time (except on days when we hold author celebrations or conduct computer labs). Some will be prewriting, some revising, some taking part in a peer conference, some editing (either alone or with a peer), some making books, some typing their stories (if the classroom has one or more computers), some having a conference with us. It's a lively hubbub, but everyone is busy. (Of course, it's a good idea to set deadlines.)

Someone, we don't remember who, has said, "The best writing teachers we have are the authors of the books we are reading." Atwell (1987) refers to this as *literary borrowing*, and we see it manifested in our writing workshops year after year. Reading becomes even more powerful when students are writing. As Calkins (1983) reminds us, "When children view themselves as authors, they approach texts with the consciousness of 'I am one who needs to know how texts are made.' Writing gives them a new reason to connect with reading." (p. 157)

What Do Writers Need?

Here are some key principles we have learned over the years:

■ *Students must be readers to be strong writers.* We pick up a piece of student writing and know immediately whether the student is a reader. Often we can even tell what they are reading, because the author's voice is recognizable in the student's writing. As students read and write at the same time, they naturally borrow the voices of the authors of the books they're reading (or that are being read to them) without realizing it.

- *Students need to write about topics they are passionate about.* We all have passions in our lives. The topics that we are most passionate about make the best writing topics. Students write best what they know best—things that have happened or are happening to them. They can be taught how to make lived experiences come to life on the page—to take the reader through the experience. We encourage students, at least at the beginning of the year, to discover and explore these passions. Prewriting activities (examples are provided in the next chapter) help students discover enough topics to get them started and stay engaged for the entire year and beyond.

- *Students need time to get immersed in their own writing.* Without time to write within the school day, students can't and won't write. Real writers set aside blocks of time to get lost in their writing. Only when our students get lost in their own writing can they get a reader of that writing to go through the experience with them. They must relive the experience on the page. Even fiction is based on experience—that of the author, someone the author knows, something the author has read about or seen on television or at the movies.

- *Students need knowledgeable teachers who are writers themselves.* Unless teachers are writers and understand their own writing process, they will not be able to help students discover and understand theirs. They will not realize the value of letting students have time to explore topics. They will not be patient with the amount of time it takes to develop a piece of writing. They won't let students write just for the sake of writing. Teachers who are writers themselves understand that if their students are writing as much as they need to be writing, they as teachers can't and don't need to read it all. They understand that their students will become better writers just by writing. They understand the need to be patient, to slow down, to not try to teach everything at once.

- *Students need daily opportunities to share their work.* Students must have time every day to share their writing. Sharing promotes more writing, gives them ideas for future pieces, provides an opportunity for them to give and receive feedback, and creates camaraderie in the classroom.

- *Students need opportunities to publish their work.* Being published promotes more and better writing. When students know their work will be read by others, they work harder. Reading one another's published work generates new ideas and prompts feedback, both proffered and received. The classroom becomes a community of writers.

What Are the Basic Components of Writing Workshop?

Writing workshop provides a structure that allows students to write every day. By writing every day, they learn to write even when they're not writing, as Donald Graves so aptly reminds us (Calkins et al. 1987). These are the basic components of the writing workshop:

- *Minilessons.* Minilessons are short lessons (usually no more than ten minutes), based on the needs of the students and presented at the beginning of writing workshop. Minilessons at the beginning of the year focus on prewriting activities that prompt students to identify topics from their lives. As the year progresses students gravitate to other kinds of writing, typically the kind of writing they are reading at the time. Throughout the year we introduce students to a variety of genres. Gradually, minilessons move into revision and conventions, always focused on one aspect of writing at a time and always based on students' needs. We encourage our students to attempt writing in different genres, the best models being the books they are reading.
- *Independent writing.* Students write on topics of their own choosing. During the first five or ten minutes, we write on our own topic to model that we are also writers. We share our writing and revisions and ask students for their suggestions about how to make our writing better. We become part of the community of writers. Students trust us more if they see us as writers who go through the same experiences the students go through. While the students are writing independently, we *confer* side by side with individual students, to assess their strengths and needs and to provide instruction and feedback based on those needs. The first conferences are content conferences in which we praise the student for something specific he has done in the writing. Maybe we begin by getting a student to extend that writing. Writ-

ing should be taught whole to part; content comes first. If a student isn't extending his writing, we don't want to focus on conventions, even if that's where we are in the minilessons. Moving too fast, focusing on conventions too soon, shuts a writer down. We must use the teachable moment, focus on one thing at a time. We never tell the student everything that is wrong with the writing. We also never take a pen or pencil to the conference. The student holds the pen.

■ *Sharing*. During the final ten minutes of a writing workshop, students share their work as a whole class, in small groups, or in pairs. Sharing is always voluntary, and students know they are safe, that their writing will not be criticized but, rather, that they will be supported as writers.

Figure 5–1 is a typical schedule for writing workshop.

MINILESSON
(10–15 minutes)

The teacher presents short writing lessons based on the students' needs. Minilessons help guide students through the writing process and teach good writing strategies and skills. Minilessons at the beginning of the year focus on prewriting activities to get the students engaged. As the year progresses, minilessons focus on revision strategies and writing conventions, always focusing on one aspect of writing at a time and always based on the students' current needs.

INDEPENDENT WRITING
(30–45 minutes)

Students write silently on topics of their own choosing, each at various stages of the writing process. During the first 5 to 10 minutes the teacher writes silently in her own writing notebook. The teacher spends the remainder of the time conferring with individual students to assess and provide further instruction.

SHARING
(10 minutes)

Students share their writing as a whole class (3 or 4 students per session), in small groups, or in pairs. Students may also evaluate and reflect on their individual learning and growth as writers.

Figure 5–1 A Typical Schedule for Writing Workshop

Some teachers ask, "But won't my students and I get bored doing the same thing all the time?" The answer is no. Even though the structure is the same, what happens within that structure is always different. The students' writing is always different, and our minilessons and conferences are based on the needs of those particular students on that particular day.

A predictable structure is critical. Students need structure. They need boundaries and clear expectations. We teach these to the students the very first week of school and spend the first several weeks strictly—and consistently—enforcing them. Once the structure is in place, we allow students the freedom to make choices about what to write, where to work, and so on. The structure creates a safe environment in which students can make choices, take risks, focus on reading and writing, and learn, learn, learn. Writing workshop keeps "stuff" from getting in the way of what really matters.

What If a Student Refuses to Write?

In the beginning of the year, students may not be convinced they can write. They may become anxious, because they don't yet know what our expectations are. They may still believe that they have to write perfect papers that are going to be turned in for a grade. And they may be afraid they will have to share their writing with others.

Once students who have been taught they can't write are expected to write, convinced that they can write, given time each day to read and write, and immersed in a community of readers and writers learning from one another and the authors of the books they are reading, they will blossom as readers and writers.

Assessing Writers Through Kidwatching

Most of what we teach in a writing workshop is generated by the needs of the students. As we watch the students during independent writing, we can tell who is engaged and who isn't:

A student has two sentences on the page: "I like Tony. He is my best friend."
TEACHER: Who is Tony?
STUDENT: He's a boy who lives on my street.

TEACHER: Where did you meet Tony?

STUDENT: He moved next door to me in September.

TEACHER: What's his last name?

STUDENT: Rand.

TEACHER: You may want to add those things to your story.

The teacher moves on, giving the student time to extend his story.

TEACHER (*later*): Oh, I see you've added a lot about Tony. Why is Tony your friend? Tell me one thing you do together.

STUDENT: We skateboard every afternoon.

TEACHER: Tell me about one afternoon when you were skateboarding with Tony.

STUDENT: (*begins to tell the story orally*)

TEACHER: Good. Put it on your paper. I'll be back.

Record Keeping

By keeping track of students' writing progress, teachers and students can continually move forward.

- *Anecdotal notes.* We keep an index card for each child in a box on the conference table. (The box has tabs for each class.) On this card, we jot down a brief note about each conference we have with a student. (Some teachers like to keep a notebook with a section for each student.) These notes document our instruction and are a handy guide for future instruction.

- *Skills I Have Learned sheet.* The students keep a Skills I Have Learned sheet (see Appendix L) in their writing folders. They bring this sheet to each conference and use it to jot down the skill that they learn that day. This becomes an ongoing, cumulative reminder for students when revising and editing future pieces and can be turned into a rubric at the end of the year.

- *Pieces I Have Written sheet.* Students also glue or staple a Pieces I Have Written sheet (see Appendix K) to the inside cover of their writing folder and keep an ongoing list of all the pieces they have written. Their progress is visible at a glance—to them and to us.

Why Does Sharing Really Matter?

When students know they have opportunities to share and publish their work, they are motivated to write more and write better. Through sharing, they discover new ideas for future topics and emulate the voices of their peers. Sharing generates a positive environment early in the year by helping students feel good about their work. It sets the tone for writing workshop, promotes better listening, and inspires mutual respect.

Students should never be forced to share, but the classroom should be run in a way that makes them feel comfortable doing so. Students writing and sharing together build a strong classroom community.

Whole–Group Share

In the beginning of the year, we like to have *whole-group shares* so we can model what happens when writers share. Students may of course remain seated at their desks or tables, but we find it more effective to gather back in the meeting area, as we have done for the introductory minilesson. To create an even more inviting space, some teachers join students on the floor in a *share circle* (Figure 5–2). Others prefer to gather students on the floor facing the *author's chair*.

We explain how this whole-group share is a place where we can come together as a community of writers to share without feeling embarrassed or scared. This is a place where we build one another up as writers by exchanging ideas, writing strategies, praise, and suggestions. We ask volunteers to share their writing, never forcing or calling on anyone to share. In the beginning of the year, some students are hesitant, but as they see how positive the environment is they begin to open up.

When a student shares, we model how to listen. Even though everyone brings his or her writing notebook to the circle (students who didn't plan to share often change their minds), we have them place their closed notebooks in front of them while others are sharing to reduce distractions and to emphasize how we give the student who is sharing our complete attention.

When a student finishes, everyone claps. Then we share things we like about the student's writing and encourage the students to add similar com-

Figure 5–2

ments. This positive feedback builds up students as writers and is an opportunity to point out good writing tools and strategies.

Whole-group shares work well throughout the year whenever we teach specific writing minilessons. Meeting as a group at the end of independent writing is a perfect opportunity to point out how individual writers applied the tool or strategy taught in the minilesson in their own writing. It also allows us to assess students' understanding of and ability to apply what they've learned and to recap the minilesson.

Small-Group and Pair Shares

There are also times when we want more students to have an opportunity to share in a smaller setting. Some students feel more comfortable sharing in small groups of students they know or with a partner. These groupings are especially effective on days when there is not as much time left at the end of class or when students just need a few minutes to share a particular technique they've used in their writing.

Pair shares are even more valuable when we teach students how to have peer conferences in order to receive feedback on their writing in progress. Students receive a specific response from a fellow writer about how to improve their writing.

What Do Students Share?

Most of the time we let students choose how and what they want to share, but sometimes we want them to share something in particular. For example, after a writing minilesson on revising leads to "hook" the readers, we might ask them to share their before-and-after versions and discuss which one sounds better. If we have been working on show, not tell, all week, we may want them to share a place in their writing where they were able to use the senses to pull the reader in. If we see that students have applied strategies from minilessons in their pieces of writing, we might ask them if we can make an overhead of their writing to use as an example of that strategy during the minilesson the following day.

As students become writers and share their writing with one another, writing workshop takes on an energetic liveliness. When students share, we learn more about their needs as individual writers and can revisit these needs in one-on-one conferences. We also learn more about the common needs of all our students and can use these for future minilessons.

How Do Students Publish Their Writing?

We must give our students opportunities to publish their work, to experience in the classroom what real authors experience in the world. Allowing students to carry pieces of writing through to publication, to be shared with and read by others, gives them an added sense of purpose. With encouragement and support from their peers, published writers experience a sense of completion and accomplishment for their hard work and growth as writers.

Author Celebrations
Allowing students to celebrate published writing in class builds a sense of community within the writing workshop. This day of celebration is typically

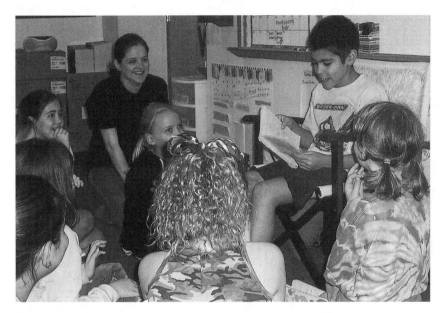

Figure 5–3

called *authors day*. It occurs about once every month or two, depending on the grade level and the length of the pieces. Each student chooses one piece to publish at a time. We teach students how to type and format their pieces neatly on the computer. We show them how to transform their typed stories into unique, creative books that look like the ones they're reading. They design covers and often add a dedication and an about-the-author page to make it look like a real published book. Bookmaking is a great way to encourage students to see themselves as real authors, and kids really enjoy the process.

On authors day the students share their individually designed books with the class one by one. They sit in the special author's chair (typically the read-aloud chair) and read their writing aloud. These books are then added to the classroom library, maybe on a special display shelf, for students in all our classes to read.

Class Anthologies

At the end of the year, each student chooses a favorite piece to go into a class or grade-level anthology. (If you have large classes and your students have written lengthy stories, you will probably want to have separate anthologies for each class you teach. Also, bonds among writers are stronger within individual classes.) The students choose a name for their anthology, an illustrator to design the cover, the colors of the pages, and so on. These anthologies are great mementos for students of all their hard work and growth as writers. Many students comment that their class anthology is just as important and special as their school yearbook.

Then we have an anthology celebration. We put the anthologies in a big box wrapped up like a present, bring it to class, and let the students unwrap the box together, which adds to the excitement of this special event and to the importance of these anthologies. Each student receives a copy. Students can exchange them, adding signatures and special notes, just as they do with their yearbooks.

Class anthologies also allow students to take their published work beyond the classroom and proudly share them with friends and family.

Prewriting Minilessons

6

Get it down. Take chances. It may be bad, but it's
the only way you can do anything really good.

——WILLIAM FAULKNER

Our first day of writing workshop finally arrives. I eagerly take my seat beside the overhead projector in the meeting area as the students anxiously trickle in, clutching fresh, new writing notebooks.

I examine their faces. Some look eager; others are doing everything in their power to avoid eye contact with me. Several girls choose spots right in front, then look up at me and smile. They sit straight and look attentive, proudly resting their writing notebooks in their laps, hoping I will notice the decorative stickers they've applied to the covers.

I smile back, giggling a little inside: these students will raise their hands to answer every question, lifting their arms as high and as straight as possible, right in my face, as if to say, Call on me! Call on me! You can't see anyone else behind my hand, so just call on me!

Two boys linger in the back of the crowd, waiting to see where everyone else is going to sit and then slowly meandering to an empty space in the far back corner—as far away from me as possible. One of them glances up at me, his look saying, Whoops! It looks like all the seats up front are taken. Guess we'll just have to sit back here. The other one looks down, exhibiting classic don't-call-on-me body language. Out of the corner of my eye I see them exchange a look: Yeah, like she's really gonna get me to write anything. Writing sucks.

I brush it off, expecting these different attitudes and energies on the first day of writing workshop and already knowing a little bit about each student's attitude toward and interest in writing from the inventories they filled out on the first day of school.

I try to meet every student's eyes with excitement and reassurance. Some look nervous. Some look anxious. Some look like they don't even know they're on planet earth. Some look like they want to go back to bed. Some look like they just rolled out of bed. Some look around the room to see who's looking at them.

Figure 6–1

Here I am, in front of thirty-four middle school girls and boys, and I have fifty-five minutes to set the stage for what is going to happen in writing workshop for the rest of the year. Fifty-five minutes to convince them that this class isn't going to be like every other English class they've had: be assigned a topic, write for a few days and turn it in, and get it back with red ink dripping off the pages.

Today I have to show them that I'm serious when I say they can write about whatever they want, and I have to help them discover all the many possible topics they can choose from in their lives. I know that if we can fill the first few pages of our writing notebooks with topics to write about, then our first day of writing workshop will have been a success and the students will be one step closer to thinking like writers.

■ ■ ■

Minilessons, based on what the students need to learn that day and presented at the beginning of writing workshop, are usually short—about ten minutes. They can, however, be longer, especially when we are introducing a new writing technique. In the beginning of the year our minilessons focus on a few good prewriting activities to help students discover topics, build fluency, and fill their writing notebooks with writing. The focus is not on conventions. Focusing on conventions too early shuts writing down. As the year progresses, the focus of the minilessons gradually shifts from discovering topics to revision, organization, and conventions. We teach one thing at a time, basing our instruction on the students' needs and level of accomplishment.

You can't just turn students loose and tell them, "Go write." You must guide them through the process of discovery. The first part of the school year is devoted to helping writers identify their passions, which make the best writing topics.

Topics I Can Write About

Borrowing from Nancie Atwell's *In the Middle* (1987, 1998), we begin the school year with a Topics I Can Write About activity to help students feel successful about writing. We walk them through it, step by step, like this:

- ■ "We will be writing every day. When you write, I will write also."
- ■ "We all have passions in our lives—things we care deeply about. They may be people who are special to us, places we have traveled, hobbies, or things we like to do in our spare time. They are topics we care about—experiences we have lived or are living. Our passions make the best writing topics."
- ■ "Something that works well for me is to list the things I care about. I knew I would be writing today, so as I was driving to school this morning I began thinking about things I feel passionate about that would make good writing topics." Write "Topics I Can Write About" on the board or overhead and begin numbering and listing as you speak.
- ■ "Who are the special people in your life? Who are the people with whom you share the most memories?"
- ■ "You can begin with your own name, because you can write about yourself. Then there are your family members. Of course, if any of these relationships don't apply to you or you don't have a significant relationship with these relatives, skip them. I'm going to start with my

mother. I called her Mama, so I'll write down 'Mama'." Continue through the following list, using actual names listed separately:

- dad
- sisters and brothers
- grandpas and grandmas
- aunts and uncles
- cousins
- nieces and nephews

■ "Who are some other people (or living beings) in your life?"

- friends
- teachers
- pets

■ "What else could you write about?" Allow time for them to respond.

■ "List places you've enjoyed visiting. Maybe somewhere you went on vacation, a visit to the mall, a trip to a friend's or relative's house, a sleepover, anything like that."

■ "What are your hobbies? If you weren't in school today, what would you be doing? What do you like to do in your spare time?"

■ "Okay, how many of you have written down at least ten topics?" Hands go up. "How many have at least twenty?" Continue until you've identified the highest number of topics, and then celebrate the wealth of topics.

■ "Look through your list and find the one topic that you want to write about today. Put a star beside it, and write that topic at the top of a clean page in your writing notebook." Model doing this using your own list on the board or overhead.

■ "Write on this topic for ten minutes. Don't worry about punctuation, capitals, neatness, or spelling. And don't stop writing. If you run out of ideas on one topic, move on to another, always writing the new topic at the top of a clean page so you'll be able to return to it later. Putting the pen down is the same as telling your brain there is nothing else to write, and your brain believes what you tell it." While the students write, write with them.

■ "Okay, finish the thought you're expressing and stop writing. Who would like to share what you've written?" As the hands go up, assign numbers. "Bring your writing notebooks to the meeting area; you may change your mind about sharing once we get started and you feel more comfortable. José, you'll be first."

- ■ "When José has finished sharing, those who would like to tell him something you liked about the piece, will raise your hands. José will call on two people." José shares his piece and then calls on two of the students who have raised hands, one at a time. Then the next person shares.

Writing workshop has begun on a positive note. Everyone has something to write about and listens closely to the work that is being shared.

For the rest of the week, the opening minilesson is short. We tell students they can write about anything they want—something on their Topics I Can Write About list, an extension of something they've already begun, or something else entirely. We ask them to write each new topic on the top of a new page in their notebook and begin freewriting. We remind them that if they run out of ideas on one topic they should choose another rather than put their pen or pencil down. At the end of each workshop we spend ten minutes sharing.

Blueprinting

Blueprinting, an activity used in the New Jersey Writing Project in Texas institute and adapted from Peter Stillman's *Families Writing* (1989), is very effective, and students like it. It can take as much as two class periods the first time it is introduced, but the time is well spent. Here's how it might play out:

- ■ "Today we're going to do another prewriting activity called blueprinting, but first we're going to make a house using this paper." Give each student a twelve-by-eighteen-inch sheet of heavy drawing paper (Figure 6–2).
- ■ "Close your eyes and think of a house or an apartment, a dwelling place that has many memories for you." Not all students have houses, and some may even be homeless. Approach this activity with sensitivity and an awareness of your students' living conditions. "It may be the house or apartment you live in now or have lived in in the past. It may be a grandparent's house, an aunt or uncle's house, or a friend's house. But it's a place that has lots of memories." Give them time to visualize. "When you have the house in mind, open your eyes."

1. Take a 12" x 18" sheet of paper.

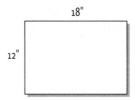

2. Turn the rectangle so that the short sides of the paper are at the top and bottom.

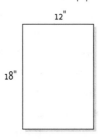

3. Fold the paper in half top to bottom.

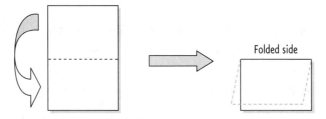

4. Find the center-point of the folded side by folding the paper in half from left to right. Don't crease the paper at this new fold. Instead simply pinch a crimp at the top of the paper to mark the center-point (where the arrow is pointing below). Then open the paper back up.

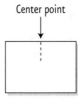

Figure 6–2 Blueprinting Activity: Constructing a House

5. Fold the left and right sides of the paper in to meet that crimped center-point. Crease these new folds.

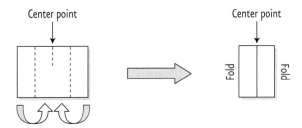

You should now have two flaps of paper meeting at the center-point—like a book jacket. (Look at the picture above on the right.)

6. Starting at the center-point, fold the top corner of the left flap back until it meets the left fold of the rectangle. It should form a tiny triangle at the top of the flap. Make a crease at this fold.

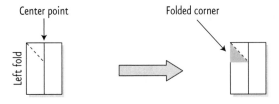

7. Now do the same to the right side. Fold the top corner of the right flap back until it meets the right fold of the rectangle. It should form a tiny triangle at the top of the flap. Make a crease at this fold.

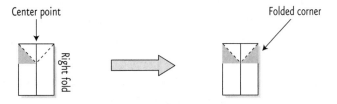

Now both top corners of each flap should be folded back. (Look at the picture above on the right.)

Figure 6–2 *Continued*

8. Now open up the left flap and fold it down so that the creased folds at the top flatten out to form a large triangle. (Your triangle should now have doubled in size.)

Left flap
(open)

9. Now do the same with the right flap. Open up the right flap and fold it down so that the creased folds at the top flatten out to form a large triangle.

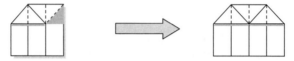

You should now have a house in front of you.

Figure 6–2 *Continued*

■ "Take your colored pencils or crayons and design the front of the house. Where are the doors? The windows? Are there trees in front or shrubs or flowers? Design the house to look like the house you have in your mind." Give them about twenty minutes to do this. It's well worth the time, because memories are being triggered. Also, if they put a lot of effort into the outside of the house, they'll work hard on the rest of the activity as well. Work on your own model house as the students work on theirs (Figure 6–3).

■ "Put your houses to one side and look at the board. Now we're going to draw a blueprint of your house's floor plan. What is a blueprint?" Give students time to respond. Bring in blueprints from home-decorating magazines or the Sunday newspaper Home section as examples. "I'm going to draw a blueprint of the house I grew up in, because it has lots of memories for me." Draw your own blueprint

Figure 6–3

on the board, labeling rooms as you go: *my bedroom, mom and dad's bedroom, living room*, etc.

- "Now I'm going to look out the window of my house. I see the walnut tree where I played as a child [draw and label the walnut tree] and the pond at the back of the house where I went fishing [draw and label the pond]."

- "Unfold your houses and, on the top of the long center section [6 inches by 18 inches], draw a blueprint of the inside of your house. If you have two floors, do two different blueprints but stay to the top of the long strip because you will be listing things below." Give students about fifteen minutes to complete their blueprints, and check their work.

- "Now watch the board again. I'm going to make a list below the blueprint for every room in the house and everything that I have labeled outside the house, leaving space under each heading to write memories. As I write down a heading, I'll brainstorm some related memories [do so], then go on to the next room. Once all the headings are listed, I can bounce back and forth between them." Model the process, thinking and talking aloud as you write things down.

Figure 6–4

- "Now make your own lists, jotting down memories under each heading." Give students about fifteen minutes to brainstorm (Figure 6–4).
- "Find a stopping place. If you haven't finished, you can list more memories later. How many have at least ten? Twenty? Thirty?" Keep going until the maximum number has been reached.
- Celebrate the number of memories students were able to generate, and tell them that each of these memories is a topic to write about, a story waiting to be written and shared.
- "Go through your lists and find the one topic you want to write about today. Put a star beside the topic. Write the topic on the top of a clean page in your notebook." Check to see that all students have written down a topic. "Freewrite for ten minutes." While the students are writing, write about a memory of your own. After ten minutes, ask students to finish their thought and stop writing.
- "Who would like to share?" As hands go up, assign each student a number. Have all the students bring their blueprints to the meeting area. The person who is number one shares. After the first student shares, have the rest of the students offer feedback on what they liked about the piece and ask any questions they have.

Once this activity has been introduced, a minilesson can be as simple and brief as reminding students where to go for their writing ideas. For the rest of the week, they choose other topics from their Topics I Can Write About lists or from their blueprints, or develop a piece they have already begun. We remind them that each time they change topics, they should begin a clean page.

Reading-Writing Connections

Reading-writing connections were first introduced to us by Joyce Armstrong Carroll and Eddie Wilson. We read a picture storybook at the beginning of writing workshop, one we think will trigger similar memories in all students. As we read, we ask them to think about these memories. Afterward, we send them back to their seats to freewrite for ten minutes. Then we ask who would like to share, call all the students back to the carpet, and let the volunteers share their writing. Some books that work well for this exercise are:

- *Roxaboxen*, by Alice McLerran
- *Bigmama's*, by Donald Crews
- *Ghost Eye Tree*, by Bill Martin, Jr.
- *My Brother's a Pain in the Backseat*, by Dale Bulla
- *Ira Sleeps Over*, by Bernard Waber
- *Too Many Tamales*, by Gary Soto
- *When the Relatives Came*, by Cynthia Rylant
- *Wilfred Gordon McDonald Partridge*, by Mem Fox
- *All the Places to Love*, by Patricia MacLachlan

A Final Word

Prewriting activities like these get students off to a successful beginning. Their writing pours out. After the first few weeks, students spend most of the workshop writing. It takes on a life of its own. The students know that they may choose what to write and that they must write something. For a good four to six weeks at the beginning of the year (depending on their prior experiences), our students just write. When they write every day, writing becomes a habit. They begin to think about writing even when they aren't in school. They see writing topics all around them (Calkins 1993). They have learned to see writing ideas everywhere and to jot those ideas down before they are lost because they are seeds for future pieces. We teach them to think and see the world like writers do.

These prewriting activities focus on memoir because we want our students to learn that the best writing comes from their own experiences. Portalupi and Fletcher (2004) remind us:

> Don Murray asserts that good writing begins with "honest, specific, accurate information." Personal narrative puts students in a realm where they can bring to the table those specific details that make the writing come alive. Personal narrative creates a tension between what you remember (what is in your head) and what you have written on the page. This tension encourages students to revise. For this reason personal narrative is a good genre in which to help beginning writers learn the cycle of craft all writers go through. Personal narrative continues to build community as students share stories that reveal their lives and allow them to learn about each other. . . . This is a genre where we can stretch students. (p. 28)

Students are eager to begin other genres, but for now we keep them focused on memoir. The best way to teach them how to take a reader through an experience is for them to write about something they have experienced.

Teachers must take into account the amount of time allotted to writing workshop each week. In ideal classrooms, where students can write every day, they are able to move on to revision more quickly than students in classrooms where time spent writing is sporadic.

Teachers must also judge when it is time to move from prewriting to revision and publication in these early stages of writing. We must allow our students to tell us when it is time to move on. We must be aware of their prior experiences with writing and their ongoing needs as writers. In classrooms where the majority of students have little experience writing about topics of their own choosing or writing for extended periods, or who complain, "I don't have anything to write about," we spend more time at the beginning of the year on prewriting to help students relax, become more fluent, and enjoy the process of writing.

In other classrooms students arrive with rich writing experiences. These students may not need to spend as much time prewriting. Their writing notebooks quickly swell with writing topics. They may be ready to move into revision and publication much sooner.

Revision Minilessons

7

The teacher who approaches teaching revision by pronouncement has the same effect on a student's writing as a politician at a national convention. Proclaiming a candidate as a "man or woman of the people" doesn't make it so. Telling isn't teaching. The uninformed, untrained teacher announces, "today you will revise your paper." Then the teacher wonders why the students did not revise. Revision must be taught in order for it to be incorporated into writing.

——JOYCE ARMSTRONG CARROLL

"Aw, man! Please don't stop reading! You can't stop there. Just one more chapter!"

Nevertheless, I close Lois Duncan's Summer of Fear *and lay it in my lap. She gets them every time—leaves them hanging at the end of each chapter, telling them just enough to hunger for more.*

Today, instead of asking what they think is going to happen next, I remark that the author has certainly gotten us worked up and involved in the story.

"Man, she's always doing that," a boy says to a friend beside him. He turns to me. "Why does she gotta do that? Man, leave us hangin' like that."

"Why do you think?" I look around the classroom, inviting everyone to join in the conversation.

One of the girls sitting up front says matter-of-factly, "She does it on purpose. She wants us to keep reading."

A few other students chime in their agreement. I ask, "What is it she's doing that makes us so involved in this book? How does she get us to this point where we want to keep reading and keep reading until we find out everything that's going to happen?"

"She ends each chapter at a really good part where you just have to know what's going to happen next."

"She ends chapters in the middle of a problem so you want to keep reading."

I ask how she pulled us in in the first place. I remind them that we wouldn't care about Rachel's problems or what she's going to do next if we didn't care about Rachel. "So what is it that Lois Duncan has done that has pulled us into this story from the beginning?"

"She's just a good writer," a boy comments in an enough-said tone.

Figure 7–1

"You're right. She is. She's one of the best young adult mystery writers I've read. But what makes her writing so good? What does she do as a writer that makes us want to keep reading?"

I see some blank faces as the students begin to ponder the question. Others immediately shoot their hands up. We begin to unravel the mysteries of good writing, to make observations about what it takes to be a good writer like Lois Duncan, to pull readers into our writing like she does so they don't want to put the book down until the last page—and even then don't want it to end.

"She makes me feel like I'm right there in the story."

"How does she do that?"

A girl recalls the place in the book where Rachel wakes up to the smell of bacon drifting up the stairs and underneath the door into her bedroom and the sunlight shining in through the window. "You could really smell and feel that."

"She gives a lot of description about what the characters look like," adds another student. "You can picture them in your mind."

"She's really good at writing problems."

As they name Duncan's techniques, I jot them down on chart paper.

This is a starting point. Today we have begun a dialogue that will continue in our writing minilessons for the rest of the week—and throughout the year. Today we have stretched our ability to think like writers. We have added new depth to the way we read.

When we have exhausted our list, I ask, "How many of you are reading a good book? Books written by authors who pull you in like Lois Duncan does?" I am surprised by how many hands go up. Even the few students who haven't yet shown a great interest in their book raise their hands, as if to say, I'm not going to get beat out by anybody. My book is as good as anyone else's.

"Today, we're going to do something special during independent reading. Instead of just reading like readers normally do, we are going to take reading one step further and read like writers. Today I'm going to give each of you some sticky notes. While you're reading, I want you to notice places in your story where your author is really pulling you in—places that make you want to keep reading, places that are intriguing—and bookmark those places. At the end of independent reading, we will share some of these places with each other. Perhaps we will be able to add to our list and continue to uncover what these good writers are doing."

■ ■ ■

There is no better way to introduce revision than by analyzing the tools authors use. The best writing teachers kids have are the authors of the books they are reading.

The day before we begin teaching revision, we invite students to look through all their writing and select one piece they want to publish. "Your stories will become published books!" We share various drafts in our own writing notebooks, thinking aloud as we narrow the possibilities and commit to one piece that we will publish.

Traditionally, teachers write comments in the margins like "vague" or "revise" or "awk," without providing any models of what those terms mean or, more important, how students can make improvements. Perhaps those teachers didn't know good writing themselves, weren't writers themselves. When teachers become writers, going through the same processes they take their students through, teaching takes on a new life. Teachers of writing must be readers who get lost in the world of the author and writers who get lost in their own writing. They must model this process for their students.

The following minilessons help take the guesswork out of revision, making it less painful for our students. Just as students need strategies for finding topics, they also need strategies for revision. We have borrowed from many sources to create a combination of strategies that help students spot weak places in their writing and show them how to do a better job at pulling the reader in.

As the vignette at the beginning of this chapter demonstrates, students begin by looking for the tools that authors use in the books they are reading, then share what they've discovered. As student volunteers read excerpts one by one, the class examines what each writer is doing and records these observations on a projected transparency, chart paper, or chalkboard under the heading Tools Authors Use. This becomes our writing minilesson for the day.

What we discover together (discovering is much more powerful than telling) is that the authors are appealing to the senses. If someone shares a passage in which the author does a great job of letting us see what the character sees, for example, we ask, "What other authors have helped you see something?" "Did an author help you hear anything?"

Joan Lowery Nixon's Three Rules for Revision

Joan Lowery Nixon, a Houston author who published well over a hundred books during her lifetime, spoke at numerous conferences during the twenty years before her death. In her early years as a writer she loved writing but hated revision. Eventually, revision became her favorite part of the process, because of three simple rules she followed:

1. She went back to the writing and found places where she could pull the reader in by making them see what she saw, smell what she smelled, taste what she tasted, hear what she heard, and touch what she touched.
2. She replaced weak verbs with strong verbs.
3. She worked on developing a lead that would quickly pull the reader in.

To introduce these rules to our students, we share a few excerpts from a Joan Lowery Nixon mystery, examining her leads, her use of the senses, and her strong verbs. Later in the year, if there is time, we use other ideas from her book *If You Were a Writer* as subjects for minilessons.

Using the Senses to Pull the Reader In

Zooming In
Barry Lane (1993) uses the analogy of a camera's zoom lens to talk about revision. Suppose we're at a football game. We can zoom out and photograph the entire football field, or we can zoom in and capture one player in action. Good

writers know when to zoom in and when to zoom out; it's an aspect of the writer's voice. There are occasions when they want to cover a large expanse of time and other occasions when authors want to explode the moment. Guess where they learn this? From reading a lot.

Prove It!

One of our favorite revision minilessons is the Prove It! strategy developed by Joyce Armstrong Carroll (2002).

- We use an excerpt from *Harry Potter and the Sorcerer's Stone,* by J. K. Rowling:
- "One of the most popular writers I can think of right now is J. K. Rowling. Who knows what she has written?"
- "How many have read a Harry Potter book?"
- "What is it about Rowling's writing style that attracts so many people of all ages?"
- "I want to share an excerpt from *Harry Potter and the Sorcerer's Stone.* How many of you have read that book?"
- "Here is a sentence from the book [uncover just the sentence on a transparency]: *It was a horrible sight.* Do you think Rowling leaves it at this?"
- "Any of you who know her writing style know that she doesn't throw a statement out there without fully describing it. What do you think she may have done?"
- "In my own writing, I like to stop and say to myself, *Maybe it was. Maybe it wasn't. Prove it!* Let's see if Rowling proved it. Let's put it to the test [uncover the rest of the quote on the transparency]:

  > It was a horrible sight. Twelve feet tall, its skin was a dull, granite gray, its great lumpy body like a boulder with its small bald head perched on top like a coconut. It had short legs thick as tree trunks with flat, horny feet. The smell coming from it was incredible. It was holding a huge wooden club, which dragged along the floor because its arms were so long.

  Did she prove it? Does her description make it better?"

- "What is happening here? What is she doing? Can you see anything? Can you smell anything? Can you touch anything? Can you hear anything? Is there another place where she could prove it? What about, *The smell coming from it was incredible*. Can you smell it? What could she have done here?"

■ "The key to good writing is taking the reader through the experience with you. Make them hear what you hear, smell what you smell, taste what you taste, touch what you touch, and see what you see."

Show, Not Tell

Show, Not Tell is a strategy in which students can apply the techniques learned from Joyce Armstrong Carroll, Joan Lowery Nixon, Barry Lane, J. K. Rowling, and the other authors of the books they are reading.

■ "Let's practice. I'm going to write a sentence and we're going to apply the Prove It! strategy." On a projected transparency, the chalkboard, or chart paper write, *My room is messy*.

■ "Is this a telling sentence? Have we proven that the room is messy? Let's put it to the test: *Maybe it is. Maybe it isn't. Prove it!* Take me through the experience using the senses and strong verbs. What do you see in this messy room? Give me some sentences."

■ As students respond, write down their suggestions; remind them to use the senses and strong verbs.

■ Someone calls out, *Clothes were all over the bed.*

■ "Let's see whether we can make that stronger without using *to be*. How about, *Clothes covered the bed and reached the ceiling.*

■ As students contribute new sentences, teach them to make them come to life by using personification (giving personal qualities to an inanimate object). For example:

  • Original sentence: *Papers were all over the floor.*
  • Revised sentence: *Papers littered the floor.*

■ Prompt students to explore the senses, such as smell, sight, or sound.

  • *Curdled milk sat in a glass on the nightstand.*
  • *Last week's pizza stared back at me from under the edge of the bed.*
  • *Roaches scampered across the rumpled paper, and rats scurried under my feet.*

■ Because students contribute quickly, their examples will probably contain shifts in tense. You can choose to let it go and save tense consistency for another day; go back and revise at the end; or revise as you go, mentioning the need to stay in the same tense. In order to encourage brainstorming, however, don't get bogged down with too much revision and too much teaching at one time.

The following paragraphs, created by two different groups of fifth graders, amplify the statement, *My room is messy.* We save them on a transparency or chart paper to use with other minilessons and provide them to students as a handout for their writing folders as examples.

Class One   Clothes were hanging off the chair, out of the drawers, and all over my bed as pillows. Old moldy chips crunch beneath my feet. Spilled milk and empty glasses lay on the dresser. Dirty smelly tube socks hang from the bed rails. Yesterday's smoothie was dripping off the clothes hanger from when I threw it at my little sister. My hands wiped the side of my dresser as dust filled my hands and a sense of moldy cheese filled my lungs. I could hear the cockroaches lurking under my bed as they munch on my old sandwich. I looked up as a fly buzzed into a spider web where other carcasses fell out. I looked down to see a tiny rat scurrying across the room. Spider webs covered my bookcases, when I screamed from all the spiders. When I turned on the fan to get the odor of the old food out, a dead rat fell off the top on to my bed. In my closet lay two dead rats and some moldy, rotten pizza. I found my little brother buried underneath a pile of socks and shoes.

Class Two   Wrinkled clothes cover my bed and droop down from the ceiling fan in my room. Stuffed animals lay thrown on the couch and on the messy, unmade bed. Candy wrappers cover the dresser. Bed sheets hang from the curtain rod. A broken lamp lays shattered, and shards of glass stick to the dirty tile floor. I hear crickets chirping from the open window. The stench from trash and musty gym socks permeates the air. The floor creaks under my feet as I trip over dirty clothes and shoes. Sand sticks to my shoes. I accidentally step on a piece of gum I was chewing on last month. Cockroaches and maggots crawl across a month-old pizza from behind the couch.

This kind of modeling takes approximately thirty minutes done all at once, which turns the minilesson into a maxilesson, but that's okay.

Replacing Weak Verbs in Students' Own Writing

It's critical that students immediately apply the techniques they are learning to the writing they are doing independently. We use another technique we learned from Dr. Joyce Armstrong Carroll called *ratiocination* (Carroll and Wilson 1993):

- Ask students to take out the draft they are going to see through to publication.
- "Let's go back and circle the *to be* verbs in your *it was a horrible sight* and *my room is messy* sentences."
- "These *to be* verbs may be clues—not always, because you never want to take out all the *to be* verbs—that you need more detail/depth or a stronger verb in your writing. What are the *to be* verbs?" Write *is, am, are, was, were, be, being, been* on the board.
- "Take your colored marker and circle these *to be* verbs in your own writing."
- Choose one sentence containing a *to be* verb, write it on the board, and demonstrate the three potentially negative aspects of a *to be* verb:
  - "It may need more depth or elaboration: apply the Prove It! strategy to find out."
  - "It may be a weak verb that you can change to a stronger verb. Take the sentence, *The rake was by the shed.* How can we use a stronger verb that makes us see that rake?" Let the students help. "How about, *The rake leaned against the shed.*"
  - "It may be a passive construction, as in the sentence, *The ball was carried by Mary.* How can we revise this sentence so that the person doing the action is the subject of the sentence?" Let the students help. "Right, *Mary carried the ball.*"
- "Of course, you may also leave the sentence as is; you just want to be sure you've considered all the options. And certainly don't take out all the *to be* verbs just to take them out; that would stifle your voice. Also, they're authentic in dialogue, because we use a lot of *to be* verbs when we talk."
- "Use a sticky note to write down possible Prove It! revisions. Remember to take your readers through the experience with you using the senses and strong verbs. Let us see what you see, hear what you hear, taste what you taste, smell what you smell, touch what you touch."

Refer back to the *my room is messy* sentences and the Harry Potter examples. "Are there any questions?"

- Give the students twenty or thirty minutes (or whatever time is available) to work on their revisions, leaving ten minutes at the end for volunteers to share.
- "Who would like to share your revision? Good, read your sentence with the *to be* verb."
- "How did you change it?"
- "Excellent! Keep that sticky note on your draft. You may decide to use this wording when you revise your piece."
- "How did this strategy work for you? What did you learn about your writing?"

We follow up on other days with a few more examples (*The man was scary looking. My friend is fun. He is nice. They were excited. I am hungry. They are tired.*) if we need to. We keep reminding our students that great writers take us through the experience with them so that we can see the scary man, experience a fun time with a friend, and so forth.

The following are some revisions made by a fifth-grade class. *B* indicates the sentence as it was initially written (before); *A* indicates the revision (after). The sentences are transcribed as the students wrote them. Although there are spelling and grammatical errors, we don't focus on editing now. The point is revision.

B: I was a little scard.
A: My hands were shaking as I waited to get my stapeles. I could smell the arom of the pepermint the nurse was sucking on. The nurse came over two me and sceezed my stomach hard as she lifted me up on the ruff plastic covered table. A chill wnet down my back as I felt how cold the table was. Suddenly I felt the fear overwhelm me.

B: But one house was empty.
A: No cars sat in the driveway. Children ceased to play. You could smell food in the oven, but no one tended it. The lights were on but no one was home. Even the radio's soft music could be heard. But noone was there to here it. The door was open, but no one cared. They were to worried about the danger that had happened. Because it had scared the

neighbor's people to the edge of their chairs. What was going to happen. That house was still as night. A silent night. A lonely night. A night of terrors.

B: He was hitting the brakes really hard and trying to turn the weel away from the ditch by know. I knew it, we were slipping on ice.

A: I could see his feet slamming up and down over and over jut pulverizing the brake pedal with his feet. He's still angrily saying "darnit, darnit" never stoping in his muttergly mad cursing sort of voice it's not something to be happy to hear even if he's yelling at Cassie because he'll be uncamable and fuming. When I say fuming I mean it he always frowns and breathes like a bull through his nose.

The following examples are revisions achieved by zooming in and exploding the moment.

B: We were all worried for nothing

A: We crawled around the soft carpet for about 20 minutes looking for someone who was downstairs, all comfortable and warm, and snuggled in a leather chair watching the TV. I can't believe we couldn't smell the buttery popcorn and hear the different sounds of the TV. I guess we just never saw her sneak downstairs after our first round, or maybe she just never even came upstairs with us, and were just imagining things.

B: I was just about to fall asleep Boom!

A: My eyes flicked in my comfortable bed. I yawend liked crazy from the long day. My eyes continued to flicker while I squished my new feather pillow that lay next beside me. My eyes shut for a good five minutes and I only woke up from a loud boom outside my room in the cold night. The only thing I could hear was the rain pat pat patting on my window seal.

B: We drove to the hospital where my dad was waiting for me and my mom. We walked inside the waiting room.

A: We drove to the hospital where my dad stood with his hand on his head. "What happened?" he asked worried. "He cracked his head open" my mom said. I could see the fear in my dad's eyes. He picked me up and brought me inside to the waiting room. I could tell he was very worried.

The following examples demonstrate how some students were able to pull the reader in simply by strengthening the verbs.

B: It was my mom motioning for me to go in.
A: My mom's hand waved rapidly around and around and she wanted me to go in. I looked up at the beast and took a deep breath.

B: There was a pause for a moment but then Ryan speaks up.
A: Aubrey and I stood frozen in horror in the silent room until Ryan decided to open his mouth and admit what he had done.

B: There was a line of little trick-or-treaters, younger than me, with happy, smily faces, anxious to go in.
A: An eager line of little trick-or-treaters lined up acting ecxited and anxious to go in.

Adverbs are another clue that verbs may be weak. Stephen King, in *On Writing* (2000), says we should take all the adverbs out of our writing: an adverb is a sign of a weak verb. (For example, *The man tiptoed* is more evocative than *The man walked quietly*.) If we strengthen the verb we won't need the adverb. We suggest that students circle the adverbs (*ly* is a clue, but it doesn't always indicate an adverb) using a different-color pen or pencil, then use them as clues to strengthen the verbs.

We like to give students handouts from these valuable revision minilessons to add to their writing folders. "The cool thing about this writing folder," we tell the students, "is that it is like a tool kit. Each handout is a tool you can use any time you're writing (or revising or editing) to help you improve." Some teachers like their students to take notes during the minilessons, but we don't. Students' notes, especially those of struggling readers and writers, aren't very effective. We prefer having our students' undivided attention during the lessons and then give them handouts as reminders.

Leads

Our leads minilesson goes like this:

- "We've talked about how good writers pull the reader in, and you guys have been working hard to apply these techniques to your writing. As a result, your writing has improved tremendously. There's something else good writers do, another one of Joan Lowery Nixon's three rules for revision, but we haven't explored it yet. You can apply all those powerful techniques in the body of your story, but if you don't grab your readers' attention in the very beginning they may never get there. I've seen some of you do this as readers. What happens when the author doesn't grab your attention on the first page?"

- A student will always say, "I don't want to keep reading it. I want to drop the book."

- "I've seen a lot of you do just that. I still do that as a reader. When I'm choosing a book, I turn to the first page and read. If it doesn't grab my attention right away, I put the book down. This is a powerful lesson for us as writers. That entry into the story is called a lead, and guess what—as writers we have about two sentences, or twenty seconds, to capture our reader's attention (Cowan and Cowan 1980), and if we don't, they are likely to put our stories down. So this is extremely important. Today I'm going to show you how some of the most popular authors do that in their books, and then we're going to examine our own leads. As I share these leads, keep your own story in mind."

- Read some examples of good leads aloud. We use examples from Nancie Atwell's *In the Middle* (1998, pp. 167–68); we like the way she takes the same story and revises the lead four different ways.

Typical

It was a day at the end of June. My mom, dad, brother, and I were at our camp on Rangeley Lake. We had arrived the night before at 10:00, so it was dark when we got there and unpacked. We went straight to bed. The next morning, when I was eating breakfast, my dad started yelling for me from down at the dock at the top of his lungs. He said there was a car in the lake.

Action: A Main Character Doing Something

I gulped my milk, pushed away from the table, and bolted out of the kitchen, slamming the screen door behind me. I ran down to the dock as fast as my legs could carry me. My feet pounded on the old wood, hurrying me toward the sound of my dad's voice, "Scott!" he bellowed again.

"Coming, Dad!" I gasped. I couldn't see him yet—just the sails of the boats that had already put out into the lake for the day.

Dialogue: A Character or Characters Speaking

"Scott! Get down here on the double!" Dad bellowed. His voice sounded far away.

"Dad?" I hollered. "Where are you?" I squinted through the screen door but couldn't see him.

"I'm down on the dock. MOVE IT. You're not going to believe this," he replied.

Reaction: A Character Thinking

I couldn't imagine why my father was hollering for me at 7:00 in the morning. I thought fast about what I might have done to get him riled. Had he found out about the way I talked to my mother the night before, when we got to camp and she asked me to help unpack the car? Did he find the fishing reel I broke last week? Before I could consider a third possibility, his voice shattered my thoughts.

"Scott! Move it! You're not going to believe this!"

■   We follow up with more examples from authors who do a great job of pulling the reader in, displayed on a projected transparency and uncovered one at a time. After reading each lead aloud, we ask questions such as, *What are you thinking? What do you want to know? What are your questions? What is the author doing here to pull you in?*

Action

Zack Freeman woke out of a deep sleep to see his butt perched on the ledge of his bedroom window. It was standing on two pudgy little legs, silhouetted against the moon, its little sticklike arms outstretched in front of it, as if it was about to dive.

Zack sat up in bed.

"No!" he yelled. "Come back!"

But it was too late. His butt jumped out of the window and landed with a soft thud in the garden bed below.

Zack stared at the window and sighed.

"Oh no," he said. "Not again."

This was not the first time Zack's butt had run away.

— Andy Griffiths, *The Day My Butt Went Psycho!*

Dialogue

"Isobel? I'm afraid we're going to have to take it off."

"Take it off, take it off," I sang, like a vamp song; but I don't think I actually did, and I know my laughter stayed locked inside my head. I think my voice did too.

"Isobel. Can you hear me?"

I didn't know. I didn't think so.

It was my leg. I went to sleep.

— Cynthia Voigt, *Izzy, Willy-Nilly*

"Did you see her?"

That was the first thing Kevin said to me on the first day of school, eleventh grade. We were waiting for the bell to ring.

"See who?" I said.

"Hah!" He craned his neck, scanning the mob. He had witnessed something remarkable; it showed on his face. He grinned, still scanning. "You'll know."

— Jerry Spinelli, *Stargirl*

The kitchen phone rang three times before Andy picked it up. "Hello?" he said.

A voice replied, "I just killed someone."

— Avi, *Wolf Rider*

Character's Thoughts

Because the things that happened to me were so strange, I know that some people will find them hard to believe. It's like when your mind slides from sleeping to waking and something takes place that's so bizarre, you tell yourself, "I have to be dreaming. This couldn't be real." Or when you jolt awake from the nightmare, and there are still unfamiliar shapes that move through your dark room, and you stare at them with wide-open eyes, knowing they can't exist and you must be awake.

There will be more questions, and I'll have to repeat the answers over and over—even to myself—so I've bought a thick, yellow, lined tablet, and I'm going to write everything that took place, beginning with the day I died.

— Joan Lowery Nixon, *Whispers from the Dead*

Here we go again. We were all standing in line waiting for breakfast when one of the caseworkers came in and tap-tap-tapped down the line. Uh-oh, this meant bad news, either they'd found a foster home for somebody or somebody was about to get paddled. All the kids watched the woman as she moved along the line, her high-heeled shoes sounding like little firecrackers going off on the wooden floor.

Shoot! She stopped at me and said, "Are you Buddy Caldwell?"

— Christopher Paul Curtis, *Bud, Not Buddy*

Emotion

The best time to cry is at night, when the lights are out and someone is being beaten up and screaming for help. That way even if you sniffle a little they won't hear you. If anybody knows that you are crying, they'll start talking about it and soon it'll be your turn to get beat up when the lights go out.

— Walter Dean Myers, *Monster*

Character Description

I clung to the heavy oak door for support, terrified of the old man seated behind the cluttered desk. His gargoyle eyes—magnified by thick, overlarge lenses—were huge, wet shimmers in a pale, shiny-bald head; and he hunched into a tight, stoop-shouldered ball as though at any minute he'd fling out moldy wings and swoop toward me. "What do you think you're doing here?" he snapped.

— Joan Lowery Nixon, *The Name of the Game Was Murder*

Setting

It was one of those super-duper-cold Saturdays. One of those days that when you breathed out your breath kind of hung frozen in the air like a hunk of smoke and you could walk along and look exactly like a train blowing out big, fat, white puffs of smoke.

It was so cold that if you were stupid enough to go outside your eyes would automatically blink a thousand times all by themselves, probably so the juice inside of them wouldn't freeze up. It was so cold that if you spit, the slob would be an ice cube before it hit the gtround. It was about a zillion degrees below zero.

— Christopher Paul Curtis, *The Watsons Go To Birmingham—1963*

Astonishing Fact

Around 10 p.m. on Friday, February 27, Gary Searle died in the gymnasium at Middletown High School. After the bullet smashed through the left side of his skull and tore into his brain, he probably lived for ten to fifteen seconds.

— Todd Strasser, *Give a Boy a Gun*

Surprise

If you are interested in stories with happy endings, you would be better off reading some other book. In this book, not only is there no happy ending, there is no happy beginning and very few happy things in the middle.

— Lemony Snicket, *A Series of Unfortunate Events: The Bad Beginning*

You don't know me.

Just for example, you think I'm upstairs in my room doing my homework. Wrong. I'm not in my room. I'm not doing my homework. And even if I were up in my room I wouldn't be doing my homework, so you'd still be wrong. And it's really not my room. It's your room because it's in your house. I just happen to live there right now. And it's really not my homework because my math teacher, Mrs. Moonface, assigned it and she's going to check it, so it's her homework.

— David Klass, *You Don't Know Me*

■ After sharing and discussing these leads, explain that often great leads don't fit neatly into a single category. Instead, they blend the techniques. Read and discuss some examples:

He saw the first tree shudder and fall, far off in the distance. Then he heard his mother call out the kitchen window: "Luke! Inside. Now."

He had never disobeyed the order to hide. Even as a toddler, barely able to walk in the backyard's tall grass, he had somehow understood the fear in his mother's voice. But on this day, the day they began taking the woods away, he hesitated. He took one extra breath of the fresh air, scented with clover and honeysuckle and— coming from far away—pine smoke. He laid his hoe down gently, and savored one last moment of feeling warm soil beneath his bare feet. He reminded himself, "I will never be allowed outside again. Maybe never again as long as I live."

He turned and walked into the house, as silently as a shadow.

— Margaret Peterson Haddix, *Among the Hidden*

Am I going to do it? Joanna asked herself.

She looked down the brightly lit mall at the blur of faces, shoppers, balancing packages, pulling young children, peering into colorful display windows, teenagers walking in twos and threes, beginning their Friday night prowl.

Of course I am, Joanna decided, a smile spreading slowly across her face. Once I get something in my mind, I always go through with it.

— R. L. Stine, *The Boyfriend*

■ Remind students that some of the best leads grab the reader's attention in the opening sentence:

John Hawks died and kept walking.

— Bentley Little, *The Walking*

The world as we knew it ended for us on a Tuesday afternoon in May.

— Lois Duncan, *Don't Look Behind You*

It was a wild, windy, southwestern spring when the idea of killing Mr. Griffin occurred to them.

— Lois Duncan, *Killing Mr. Griffin*

My name is India Opal Buloni, and last summer my daddy, the preacher, sent me to the store for a box of macaroni-and-cheese, some white rice, and two tomatoes and I came back with a dog.

— Kate DiCamillo, *Because of Winn-Dixie*

■ "Open the book you are reading and examine the technique the author uses. It may be the first paragraph. It may be the opening line.

It may be one of the categories we have already discussed. It may be a new category. Whose author did a great job of pulling you in?"

- Let volunteers share the lead from their book, and discuss each one, discovering what the author does to hook readers and what unanswered questions readers have to make them want to read on.
- Give students handouts containing the sample leads for their writing folders.
- Give them large sticky notes and send them back to their desks to revise the lead in the writing they have chosen for publication. "A good lead leaves you with questions so you'll want to keep reading. Read through the entire piece to see whether something might be nestled in it later on that you can bring forward for the lead—maybe a piece of dialogue or an action. A good story begins with a problem. Go to where the problem develops and see whether you can use that as your lead and then perhaps continue with a flashback."
- Read one of your own stories and let the students help you apply different kinds of leads to see which one works best.
- Let the students work on their leads during the remainder of the workshop.
- Have them share their lead revisions with a partner first, then with the whole class.

Here are some examples of student leads, before (B) and after (A) revision.

B: "Honey wake up, honey wake up," my mom chanted in my ear.

A: "Aaaagh," I yelled as a dark shadow hovered above me. "Shhh," the shadow whispered. Ideas raced through my mind. What if it's a kidnapper I thought. What if he takes me away to his dark van and I never return. "Aaaagh," I screamed again. I looked at my bedroom door and I saw a smaller shadow walk to my door and turn on the lights. I gazed at the shadows and I never would expect who was standing right in front of me.

B: One day I went over to my friend's house. When I got there I found his little brother Will making block towers and destroying them.

A: Like everyone knows the little sibling gets away with everything, but this time he got caught going a little too far.

B: "One, two, three, four,—eight nine ten," my sister "cheat" counted. "Here I come!" I squeezed my nimble body further down under the cramped window seat so she couldn't find me.

A: "Kendall!" my mom yelled at a very high tone. I knew I should ditch our hide and seek game and go see what I did this time.

B: It was a late Friday night, and I had just gotten back from my baseball game. As usual my two brothers were being stupid and obnoxious.

A: Brothers, don't you ever feel how annoying they can be? Trust me. I have two of those creatures. I've learned to see their good side over the years, but don't you ever get that feeling like God, kill me now? It's stuck on me. Actually, I don't know if I'll ever be able to get it off.

B: "Yes!" It was finally the end of the night and I was dead tired.

A: The lights flickered off. "Boom woosh bam" thunder clapped and the wind rushed by. Hail outside was falling at probably 20 miles per hour. Rain crashed on the ceiling. Trees outside shook. A storm was coming soon, I could feel it.

Conclusions

After we've given students several days to work with and share their revised leads, it's time to move on to conclusions. Again, we gather examples from real books. We read the lead and then the conclusion, discussing how the two tie together and the effectiveness of this technique (Carroll and Wilson 1993).

■ "One of the most popular conclusion techniques is one which Jackie Gerla, a colleague, in oral presentations refers to as "full circle." The story ends at the same point or in the same way it began. Carroll (2004) calls it "The Call Back." Here are some examples:

Lead
I never had a brain until Freak came along and let me borrow his for a while, and that's the truth, the whole truth. The unvanquished truth is how Freak would say it, and for a long time it was him who did the talking. Except I had a way of saying things with my fists and my feet even before we became Freak the Mighty, slaying dragons and fools and walking high above the world.

Conclusion

So I wrote the unvanquished truth stuff down and then kept on going, for months and months, until it was spring again, and the world was really and truly green all over. By the time we got here, which I guess should be the end, I'm feeling okay and remembering things. And now that I've written a book who knows, I might even read a few.

No big deal.

— Rodman Philbrick, *Freak the Mighty*

Lead

Our teenage daughter Kaitlyn was chased down and shot to death while driving home from a girlfriend's house on a peaceful Sunday evening.

Conclusion

". . . But the one thing we're absolutely sure of in our own minds is that this was not a random shooting—Kait was *assassinated*."

— Lois Duncan, *Who Killed My Daughter?*

Lead

The dream is too long. It slithers and slips and gurgles deeply into midnight pools in which I see my own face looking back. It pounds with a scream that crashes into earth-torn caverns and is drowned; it surges with the babble of voices that splash against my ears; it whispers over words I can't understand. . . .

I gasp as my hands feel breasts that are rounded and firm. My shaking fingers slide past my waist, exploring, as the horror grows. I lift my head to look down, down at toes that lump the blanket near the foot of the bed, and the horror explodes in a scream. I am Stacy McAdams. I'm only thirteen years old, and I'm in the wrong body!

Conclusion

My cheek glows from the warmth of his skin through his shirt, and I can hear the steady beat of his heart. I put my arms around him. I'm Stacy McAdams. I'm seventeen. And I'm definitely in the right body.

— Joan Lowery Nixon, *The Other Side of Dark*

Lead

The thing that happened, when finally it happened, was so perfectly logical that it should not really be considered surprising. Because the fact is that even earlier in life Aremis Slake had often escaped into the subway when things got rough above ground. He kept a subway token in his pocket for just that emergency, and the emergencies kept occurring due to a joining of hostile circumstances.

Conclusion

He turned and started up the stairs and out of the subway. Slake did not know exactly where he was going, but the general direction was up.

— Felice Holman, *Slake's Limbo*

Lead

It's cold. It's late. I'm trapped in here, trying to sleep under this sorry excuse for a blanket, and I've just got to tell you—you don't know squat. You think you know what I'm going through, you think you know how I can "cope," but you're just like everybody else: clueless. Writing. Poetry. Learning to express myself. "It'll help you turn the page, Holly. Just try it."

Well, I'm trying it, see? And is it making me feel better? NO! Giving me this journal was a totally lame thing to do. You think writing will get me out of here? You think words will make me forget about the past? Get real, Ms. Leone!

Words can't fix my life.

Words can't give me a family.

Words can't do jack.

You may be a teacher, Ms. Leone, but face it: You don't know squat.

Conclusion

While I'm at it, let me confess that there *is* something to the whole poetry thing you pushed on us. I hate to admit it, but I've grown to like it. I think in stanzas sometimes. I play with phrases in my mind. It's not the sissy stuff I used to think it was. It's the raw heart of the matter.

So after mulling it over for a long time, I've decided to take Meg's advice.

I want you to know that I'm okay.
I want you to know that you helped me.
And I want to say thank you.
Thank you for helping me turn the page.

— Wendelin Van Draanen, *Runaway*

- "Now look back at the conclusions to some of the books you've already read. How do they relate to the lead?"
- "Look at the piece you are going to publish. How might you relate the conclusion to your lead?"

Paragraphing

All students need tools for organizing their writing. Paragraphs convey meaning and should come out of the writing. They cannot be predetermined. Many students have a misconception about paragraphs because of the way they have previously been taught. For too long writing instruction focused on a formula: a thesis statement and a predetermined number of topic sentences, each presented and developed in a separate paragraph (in many cases with a set number of lines!).

- "What do you know about paragraphing? How do you know where paragraphs go?"
- "A long time ago writers wrote without paragraphs." Show students a facsimile of a section of an old manuscript that has no paragraphs. "The idea of the paragraph actually emerged as a result of a little mark [¶] that the writer placed in the margin signaling the person setting the type to leave a block so that someone could later insert an illumination (maybe leaves with a fancy letter)." (Carroll and Wilson 1993)
- "Take out the book you are reading and look for places where the writing stops in the middle of a line, returns to the next line, and indents." Give students time to do this. "What are these indentions called? Why did the authors indent in these places?"
- Ask for volunteers to share a few examples of paragraphing from their books.

- "All right, let's generalize: come up with some rules for paragraphing. Authors paragraph when there is some kind of change:

  > A different speaker. (Dialogue.)
  >
  > The passage of time. (Now the character is going to bed and now he is getting up.)
  >
  > A different place. (A character is at school and then he is walking into his home.)
  >
  > A new subject/topic/action. (A character is talking about baseball. Then he starts to talk about homework.)"

- "After text has gone on for six or seven lines, we need to look for a place to break. Paragraphs can be shorter or longer, but this is a general rule of thumb. Any convention, including paragraphs, is meant to aid the reader, make the writing more reader friendly."

- Type a page from the book you are currently reading aloud, without paragraphs. Project it onto a transparency and read it aloud, so that students have time to think about it before splitting up into pairs or small groups.

- Have the pairs or groups determine where they think the paragraphs go and put the ¶ symbol in appropriate places on their own copies of the transparency.

- Ask volunteers from different groups to project their revised texts and share the thinking behind their decisions. Students will inevitably mark the paragraphs differently, sometimes justifiably, sometimes not.

- Show students how the author paragraphed the page. This will generate a lively discussion in which students discover that paragraphs can work in different places, depending on how you read and understand the flow of the story. (The author, however, has the ultimate say, because he or she understands the story best.)

- Show students the first chapter of *Holes*, by Louis Sachar. "Paragraphs can be subjective. An author chooses where to put the paragraphs depending on how he wants the reader to read the story. Paragraphs are a way for the author to walk readers through the story without having to be there in person to read it aloud to them. Paragraphs give the story voice—they show the reader how the author intends for it to sound. Some authors like longer paragraphs. Some like shorter paragraphs."

- ■ "Can the single word *Julia* be a paragraph?" Give the students a chance to share their opinions. "Yes, it can. Lois Duncan uses it that way in *Summer of Fear*, for emphasis, to slow the reader down."
- ■ "Take a colored marker, read through your draft, and decide whether you have paragraphed it in a way that will help readers understand your writing better. Just as punctuation conveys meaning, paragraphs also convey meaning."

Again, we don't teach another major minilesson this week but rather use the time to confer with students individually, helping them paragraph their own writing. (We also let them confer with each other in pairs or groups.)

A Final Word

The minilessons in this chapter introduce the tools authors most often use for revision. Remember, a few good minilessons go a long way. By slowing down the process, students have time to play around with and internalize the techniques they learn. During our conferences we can remind students about these techniques and demonstrate them individually. As students learn to emulate the authors of the books they read, these authors truly become their best writing teachers.

Editing Minilessons

8

In view of the widespread agreement of research studies based upon many types of students and teachers, the conclusion can be stated in strong and unqualified terms: the teaching of formal grammar has a negligible or, because it usually displaces some instruction and practice in actual composition, even a harmful effect on improvement in writing.

— RICHARD BRADDOCK, RICHARD LLOYD-JONES, AND LOWELL SCHOER

"Hey, Miz, I can't breathe!" a boy finally shouts from the back of the room. "Whatcha tryin' to do? Kill us?"

The rest of the class, after a unison intake of breath, bursts into giggles. Students who have caught on to my mischievous plan look at this boy as if to say, You don't know what she's trying to do? Duh! *Others look at me in confusion.*

We are in the middle of choral-reading an excerpt from our read-aloud, waiting for the author's cue to take a breath but finding none since I have removed all the punctuation marks.

I turn his question back to him: "No, I have no plans to kill you today—just to show you something. What do you think I'm trying to do?"

The look on his face says he gets it: "You're tryin' to tell us we need to breathe when we read. We can't breathe when reading this thing!"

"And why can't you breathe?"

"'Cause there's no punctuation," he says accusingly, as if telling the author, Shame on you!

"So what is the purpose of punctuation?" I watch the students' faces as they mull this over. Naturally, a few hands shoot up immediately. These students knew where I was going as soon as I projected the transparency. Slowly, other hands inch up into the air. I call on a boy whose hand is propped halfway up and whose face looks uncertain but willing to take a chance.

"What do you think?" I ask him with a nod, trying to reassure him that his thoughts will be validated, no matter what.

He responds hesitantly, "To tell the reader where to take a breath, I guess?"

"You're right," I congratulate him. I turn to the rest of the class. "You are the experts on your pieces of writing. Only you know where you want the reader to pause. Where you want the

99

Figure 8–1

reader to stop. Where you want the reader to ask a question. Where you want the reader to read
with excitement. When you read your paper to the class or a partner or a small group, you
include your pauses, your stops, your questions, your exclamations. When you are not there to
read to your audience in person, you must do that with punctuation. That's the purpose of punc-
tuation—so the reader knows how to read your writing."

"Aw, Miz, why didn't nobody tell me that before?" the boy in the back says in exasperation.
Why didn't anyone tell him this before? That's a very good question.

■ ■ ■

Many students in the older grades have spent year after year in traditional English classrooms adding punctuation marks to pointless
worksheets filled with sentences written by someone else. Many of
them have never had an opportunity to apply these skills in a meaningful context. The writing process movement taught us better than this. The best way
to teach these skills is through the context of writing. Then, and only then,
will students "own" punctuation, because it is their text, something they have
spent hour upon hour composing, and, by golly, they want it read correctly.

However, in today's high-stakes testing environment, more and more
schools are reinstituting scope-and-sequence charts that require teachers to
teach editing skills in the "correct" order. There are fewer summer writing

institutes for teachers. There is less writing in classrooms and more work-sheets and exercises out of the grammar book or, worse, sample test passages focusing on isolated skills.

If students discover examples of conventions in their reading and then apply these conventions in their own writing, the knowledge gained is more likely to stick. When teachers from elementary grades through high school advanced-placement classes are asked, "What errors do you see in your students' writing?" the answer is always the same: run-on sentences, subject-verb agreement, punctuation, capitalization, paragraphing, and spelling. That's not a long list. If we slow down, teach one skill at a time, and give students time to apply it in their own writing, the learning will be more meaningful and longer-lasting for students.

Connie Weaver's (1996a) cogent summary on the subject, entitled "On the Teaching of Grammar" may be found almost in its entirety at www.ncte.org/library/files/About_NCTE/Issues/teachgrammar.pdf. After an extensive review of the research, Weaver concluded that the systematic and formal study of grammar, such as identification of parts of speech and the parsing or diagramming of sentences, has consistently shown negative results on improving the quality of writing or language expression. On the other hand, results demonstrated that discussing grammatical constructions, usage, and punctuation in the context of writing and editing is more helpful than studying formal grammar and the rules of punctuation through isolated skills instruction. Results also concluded that extensive reading significantly promotes the acquisition of grammatical structures and grammatical fluency, especially for second language learners.

Weaver suggests the following implications for teaching grammar as an aid to writing:

- Teach only grammatical concepts critically needed for editing writing.
- Teach these concepts through minilessons and conferences, while helping students edit.
- Give students plenty of opportunities and encouragement to write, write, write for a variety of purposes and real audiences.
- Give students plenty of opportunities and encouragement to read, read, read.
- Read aloud to students, choosing at least some selections that have more sophisticated sentence structures than what the students would ordinarily read by themselves.

We present whole-class minilessons on recurring grammar problems in student writing, supplementing these lessons with instruction (as a class or in individual conferences) on less common problems as needed. For example, if a student is experimenting with dialogue before we've presented a minilesson on how to punctuate dialogue, we use a conference to teach him how to do it. Or if a number of students need to learn a particular skill, we teach them that skill as a group. Also, many students need one or several one-on-one conferences before they grasp the concepts taught in the general minilessons. And we always refer the students to the books they are reading. Authors are still their best teachers.

Run-On Sentences

When students begin to write with voice and complexity, they don't always know how to punctuate that writing, even though they may have punctuated sentences on worksheets or had their writing "corrected" by their teachers. Teaching punctuation from the perspective of *I am the only one who can tell my reader how to read this story* takes it to a new level.

Punctuation gives writing the author's unique voice. Jamie follows the scenario that opens this chapter by having the students punctuate the passage to reflect how they think the author would read the piece. Then they look at the punctuation the author used. Discrepancies lead to discussions about how punctuation conveys meaning.

Here's an excerpt from *Baby,* by Patricia MacLachlan:

Sometimes she dreamed of white hair like silk touching her face and tiny white stones tumbled beach stones maybe and crying she could almost taste the salt of tears when she thought of it the taste of memory why then wasn't she frightened when she remembered this

If a student turned in this paper, what would we do? Too often teachers grab a pen and edit away, sure they know what the writer intended but losing the writer's voice in the process. Teachers have expertise, yes, but they haven't the right to tamper with a student's voice. Here's what needs to happen: the student must read the piece while the teacher explains how to punctuate it so that others can read it in that same voice. The student holds the pen, the teacher and student together hold the piece. If Patricia MacLachlan were sitting side by side with you in a conference and she read her piece to you, perhaps you could help her use punctuation to reveal her voice, like this:

> Sometimes she dreamed of white hair, like silk, touching her face, and tiny white stones that tumbled. Beach stones, maybe. And crying. She could almost taste the salt of tears when she thought of it; the taste of memory. Why, then, wasn't she frightened when she remembered this?

Since we know what our students are reading, we have a good idea where their voice is coming from. They borrow from the books we read aloud to them and from the books they read on their own. This is not a bad thing, and we need to celebrate it instead of condemning it. Attempting to teach voice in lessons totally isolated from student writing doesn't work. Students who read write with voice, but they need us, the experts, to help them punctuate it.

We don't teach anything else this week. We *do* confer with students individually during writing workshop, helping them check for run-on sentences. If a student consistently lets her sentences run on, we ask her to read what she's written. Typically, she'll stop where the periods would be and pause where the commas would be, even though these marks don't appear on the paper. We say, "You stopped there. What do you need to do in your writing to tell the reader that you want him to stop?" "Oh," the student says and adds the period. Or, "You raised your voice there like you are asking a question. How do you tell your reader that is what you want her to do?" Or, "You said that with excitement in your voice! How do you tell your reader to read it that way?" If more support is needed, we choral-read from the book the student is currently reading, drawing attention to ending punctuation.

General Punctuation

Here's a follow-up minilesson:

- Ask students to punctuate this sentence: *Tom Smith called Sarah Lou is here*
- Ask volunteers to share how they think the sentence should be punctuated and then read it aloud.

- Demonstrate that there is no single correct way to punctuate the sentence. "How many ways do you think there are to punctuate this sentence?" (There are over seventy; see Carroll and Wilson 1993.)
- Point out that there are *incorrect* ways to punctuate the sentence, however.
- Remind students that punctuation conveys meaning and that they are the experts on their own writing.

Commas

When we focus on commas, we ask students to look in the books they are reading for examples of where authors use commas. One by one the students share what they've found, and as a class we generalize comma rules, which we post on a large sheet of chart paper, along with examples. Four basic comma rules take care of most of the comma errors in student writing (Carroll and Wilson 1993):

1. After a long introductory clause. Example: *After I went to the store to get milk, I went home.*
2. To separate an appositive. Example: *Ms. Mazy, the dentist, came to visit.*
3. To separate words in a series. Example: *I went to the store to get milk, eggs, and bacon.*
4. In a compound sentence. Example: *I went to the store, and I got milk.*

Of course, students will also discover commas in other places. The most common is in dialogue (*I said, "I'm going to the store." "I'm going to the store," I said. "I'm going," I said, "to the store."*) For the rest of the week, at the beginning of writing workshop, we ask whether anyone has found an example in their reading of a comma used in a way that we haven't discovered yet. We add these discoveries to the original chart. Again we confer individually with many students more than once. A common error is to overgeneralize and put a comma before every *and*: *I'm going to the store, and get apples.* We teach the difference between a compound sentence and a compound predicate and why the first requires a comma and the second does not.

Punctuating Dialogue

Punctuating dialogue is not easy. If students are readers, they will use dialogue in their writing long before they know how to punctuate it. Again, we refer them to the books they are reading for examples.

Figure 8–2 is an example of a transparency and handout we use when introducing students to quotation marks. The sentences were taken from Peg Kehret's *The Ghost's Grave* (2005). We like to use a book the students are familiar with. The read-aloud book works well for this. We project the transparency and discuss the rules and examples.

We then have students examine how their own authors have punctuated dialogue. We then invite them to share in pairs or small groups.

We also project the following sentences on a transparency or write them on the chalkboard:

Veronica said her mom was going to the store.
Veronica said, "Her mom was going to the store."
Veronica said, "My mom is going to the store."

We discuss the differences, explain quotations, and point out how quoted speech goes inside quotation marks. As students begin to analyze quotations

---

1. Each time a new character speaks, a new paragraph should begin.
2. Everything a character says should be in quotation marks.

> Willie looked annoyed. "If you must know," he said, "a ghost becomes an angel when he's ready to move on. That's when you get the wings and the halo."

3. Use a comma to separate an explanatory phrase from the quotation.

> Aunt Ethel said, "Here we are."
> "Here we are," Aunt Ethel said.

4. Place an exclamation mark, question mark, period, or comma inside the quotation mark.

> "Fleas and mosquitoes!" Aunt Ethel cried.
> "Do you live around here?" I asked.
> "I'm looking for my seat belt."
> "I'm looking for my seat belt," I said.

(Adapted from Geye 1997)

Figure 8–2 Rules for Punctuating Dialogue

in their reading and in their writing, they pay more attention to how authors use quotations. Again, authors are the best teachers.

Capitalization

We teach capitalization at the beginning of sentences when we teach students how to punctuate run-on sentences. Later we introduce students to the other major rules of capitalization by having them look in the books they are reading for examples and generating a list on chart paper, which we post on the wall of the classroom:

- Proper nouns (names of people and places).
- Major words in titles of books, stories, plays, etc.
- Titles of people.

They will run across other examples in their reading, which they can add to this list as appropriate.

Subject/Verb Agreement

Subject/verb agreement is a particular problem for students who don't read and write enough, because there isn't a good way to "teach" it other than by immersing students in conversation, the daily-read aloud, and independent reading. Writing and reading must be meaningful. When students are read to and given large blocks of time in which to read and write, they learn subject/verb agreement. They don't learn it by listening to lectures, filling in worksheets, or doing drills from the grammar book (Weaver 1996a; Krashen 2004a).

Spelling

Stephen Krashen (2004b) contends spelling instruction on its own has little effect. Spelling is visual and develops naturally as students read, write, and publish, and the ability to spell correctly derives from seeing words in print; in the beginning we need to allow students to use inventive spelling (phonetic spelling) (Gentry 1987; Weaver 1996c). Weaver (1996c) concludes:

For decades, more people seem to have considered themselves poor spellers than good spellers, despite the fact that most of us spell correctly the vast majority of the words we write. With spelling, we seem to expect that all of us should spell one hundred percent correctly, even on first drafts, and even as young children. Perhaps it is this unrealistic expectation that leads some parents and others to object when teachers use newer methods of helping children learn to spell, such as encouraging children to use "invented spelling" in their early attempts to write. Such critics mistakenly assume that children who initially use invented spelling will never become good spellers, or that if the time-honored method of memorizing spelling lists were used instead, every child would become a perfect speller. Neither observed experience nor research supports these assumptions. (p. 1)

Even though Weaver's conclusions are based primarily on observations of young children, they also apply to English language learners and inexperienced writers. Her analysis of the research clearly demonstrates that young children allowed to use invented spellings in their writing—as opposed to those who are only allowed to use correct spellings—employ a considerably greater variety of words to their writing, score as well or better on standardized tests of spelling, and develop word recognition and phonics skills earlier. Analysis of the research has consistently demonstrated that we can help children learn to spell by:

- encouraging learners of all ages to write, write, write and spell words the best they can in first drafts;
- helping students write the sounds they hear in words (i.e., invented spellings). Young children or inexperienced writers may begin with one sound per word, naturally progress to more sophisticated invented spellings, and then move to conventional spellings.
- encouraging learners of all ages to read, read, read;
- encouraging students to circle words in their first draft that they think may be spelled incorrectly;
- Teaching children strategies for correcting spelling:
  - writing the word two or three different ways and deciding which one "looks right"
  - locating the correct spelling in a familiar text or in print displayed in the classroom
  - asking someone

- consulting a dictionary
- using a spell-checker, the computer, or a handheld electronic speller
- learning spelling strategies and major spelling patterns through minilessons and student discussions
- noticing generalized spelling patterns
- discovering meanings of Latin and Greek roots and suffixes (intermediate and middle grades)
- Making individualized spelling dictionaries (booklet, file box with index cards, or computer files).

Atwell (2002) has some excellent suggestions for independent word study: ask students to select five words a week from their writing that are giving them trouble; have them study the five words; then have them, in pairs, test each other. Students become excited about spelling when they are free to choose the words they want to learn.

Richard Gentry, a leading spelling authority, is himself a poor speller. He has spent a lifetime teaching us the value of early experimentations though invented spelling and the stages of spelling development. He dedicates his book *Spel . . . Is a Four-Letter Word* (1987) to a college professor who called him into his office and accused him of being lazy because of his poor spelling. In his writings, Gentry emphasizes that poor spelling does not signify a lack of intelligence. Our students need to know this. Spelling comes easy for some. For others it doesn't. Some have the talent; others do not. Even though research has shown that spelling improves through reading and writing for the majority of our kids (Weaver 1996c, Krashen 2004a), there are some who find spelling a challenge no matter how much they read and write. These students are the exception. (And these days, they have the great boon of spell-checker!)

A Final Word

Grammar and mechanics, including spelling, will improve as students spend large amounts of time reading and writing. They will also improve as we teach these skills, in minilessons and one-on-one conferences, in the context of the students' own writing, one teachable moment at a time. Students learn more when we slow the process down. When students begin to experiment with conventions (punctuation, capitalization, spelling, and so forth) in their writing, they will begin to see those conventions everywhere. That's how we learn. We learn best when we have an interest in learning. We learn best when the learning is meaningful.

Conventions have only one purpose: to make writing more readable to those who want to read it. Learning how to use the proper conventions must be meaningful, timely, and take place within the context of making our own writing better. Students are more interested in making writing better if they have audiences for their writing. We can help them find those audiences by providing opportunities for students to publish their work. Publishing their work makes them care more about what they say and how they say it.

SECTION III
Getting Down to Basics

America's teachers and children don't need national committees to grade their worth. We need local teachers to reflect on their own experiences, to figure out how the students, the curriculum, and even the bureaucracy interact in a process we call education. The essence of being a teacher is knowing who you are, where you are—and liking what you find. Being a teacher means being able to draw your own map—instead of relying on mass-produced tourist guides. Being a teacher means understanding that the best map you draw still is not the territory.

— Susan Ohanian

Launching the
Workshop Classroom

Time for independent writing—and reading—isn't the icing on the cake, the reward we proffer senior honors students who've survived the curriculum. Writing and reading are the cake. When we make time, giving students one of a writer's basic necessities, we begin to make writers. . . . If we want our adolescent students to grow to appreciate literature, another first step is allowing them to exert ownership and choose the literature they will read.

—Nancie Atwell

A well-organized classroom is essential to making reading and writing workshop run smoothly. Especially in the beginning of the year, you want to make sure everything is set up and ready so that when the students walk in the door, you can focus on getting to know them and teaching them. Naturally, you will tweak the organization and setup slightly from year to year, depending on your particular school and classroom and your own and your students' personalities. This is okay. You have to make your classroom organization work for you.

How Do I Organize the Workshop Classroom?

Reading and writing workshops require the following classroom areas:

- a classroom library
- a group meeting area
- student work areas

- a conference area
- a materials center
- teacher space
- (ideally) a computer publishing center

Each area should be separate from the others, but you should be able to see into all of them for management and monitoring purposes. For example, many teachers have a meeting area in one corner or on one side of the classroom, the independent work area (desks and/or tables) in another corner or on another side. Sometimes low bookshelves, cabinets, or benches enclose the meeting area. The library, the computer publishing center, the materials center, and teacher space may be off in various corners.

For practical purposes, the areas may need to be integrated. Because older students and their desks are bigger and their class sizes generally larger, some teachers solve space issues by putting the desks or tables in a U-shape around the meeting area, so that chairs are easily accessible during a minilesson. Some teachers position rows of desks facing each other on opposite sides of the classroom, leaving a wide walkway in between that serves as the meeting area. Some teachers integrate their library and materials center into the meeting area by placing low bookshelves along the edges of the carpet. Some teachers find it easier or less distracting to hold conferences where the students are working, rather than designating a separate conference area. Choose what works best for you and your students, as long as you begin the school year with a classroom layout that allows what really matters to happen.

Understanding the function of each area will better enable you to create a classroom layout that works well for you and your students.

Classroom Library

The library is the soul of the workshop classroom, a print-rich environment where students can immerse themselves in good books and reading. Even though your school probably has a school library, students need immediate access to books, especially when they finish a book in the middle of class or need your help picking out a book that is just right. These books come in handy for you too, as examples during your teaching.

The library should be filled with books of various levels and genres, both fiction and nonfiction, books that will appeal to all students' abilities and

Figure 9–1

interests. It should include informational books about various subjects and people and reference materials such as dictionaries, encyclopedias, thesauruses, and writing handbooks and guides. If possible, bring in newspapers and magazines as well. (Scholastic publishes a handful of student magazines full of fiction and nonfiction.)

The library should be organized so that students can easily find books that are right for them. Alphabetize books on the shelves by the author's last name, grouping each genre separately. Books by the same author or in the same series or in the same genre can be put in clearly labeled and easily reachable baskets. Book baskets are a great way to highlight a particular author or genre, new books, or recommended books (Figure 9–2). You could also use a basket for resource and reference books or books that you've used as examples in your minilessons. Baskets make the space seem cozy as well. (If you can't afford real baskets, just wrap some cardboard boxes in contact paper or gift wrap, or place your book groupings on clearly labeled bookshelves.)

Figure 9–2

Let the students "own" the classroom library. Ask them to help you decide how to organize it. Create a system for keeping it organized that works for you. Ideally, using the library could be left to the honor system, but that often proves difficult. As much as you'd like the students to keep the books for as long as they wish, even permanently, you need to know who has which book when, and small budgets necessitate that books remain in the classroom year after year.

Some teachers have sign-out clipboards on which the students write their name, the title of the book they are checking out, and the date. When a book is turned in, the name is crossed off the list. However, as the number of books in your library grows, you may find it more manageable to place a library card (indicating author and title) and pocket in the back of each book. When a student wants to check out a book, he or she takes the card out of the back pocket, fills out his or her name and the date, and places the card in a tray or basket labeled Book Check-Out or Library Card Drop-Off. You can then collect all the cards at the end of the day and organize them alphabetically by author's last name, perhaps keeping your various classes separate. An index-card box with color-coded class dividers makes the job of organizing library cards easier (Figure 9–3).

It's also helpful to have a designated "book drop" (we use a brightly colored plastic crate) where students turn in their books when they finish them or have been given permission to abandon them (Figure 9–4).

Creating a check-out-and-return system may sound like a lot of extra work, but it makes it very easy to re-card and re-shelve books or to find out who has what book at any given moment. Some teachers use volunteer library assistants—students who come in before or after class and keep the library organized—or make library maintenance a duty of the classroom manager (a job that rotates from student to student week by week). We've even had students from past years ask to come in before school and after school to work in the library. Once they feel a part of the workshop classroom, they don't want to leave!

To acquire library cards and pockets, ask your school librarian if she or he has extras you could have, or borrow a supply catalogue and order them your-

Figure 9–3

Figure 9–4

self. You could also order them online from companies like Demco or find them at a nearby teacher supply store.

Don't panic if you are just beginning and don't have *any* books. The students can also bring books from home, the public library, or the school library. Take them to the school library once a week (or once every other week if you're really pressed for time). Take the index cards on which you have noted students' interests with you. Being able to go to a shelf and say, "I've found a book that I think you are going to love!" shows a student that you care. (In many schools, students are also allowed to go to the library on their own before or after school and sometimes during their lunch break.)

However you manage it, giving your students access to books is critical. Here are some ideas for building a classroom library:

- Ask your administrator for money—it never hurts to try.
- Check with your PTA or PTO organizations. They sometimes have money for teachers to use for things like books.

- Go to garage sales.
- Check local bookstores. The Half-Price Books chain donates books to teachers, and most bookstores provide discounts for teachers. Check out Barnes & Noble, Borders, or your local independent bookstores.
- Use book clubs. Teachers earn bonus points from the books their students purchase through book clubs. Those points can then be used toward free books for the classroom library. (Go to www.scholastic.com for details.)
- Locate the Scholastic Book Fair warehouses in your area. Twice a year, in December and May, they hold half-price shopping days.
- Contact the book distributors for your district. They offer greater discounts for teachers. (Richardson's Books, a huge wholesale warehouse in Houston, Texas, offers a 35 percent discount for teachers. Check it out at www.richardsonsbooks.com.)
- Write a note to parents asking them to take their children to the public library in order to check out books to read in school. We've taken our students on field trips to the public library at the beginning of the year; the students meet the librarians, take a tour of the facilities, listen to book talks on all the latest and best titles, and turn in library card application forms that their parents prepared ahead of time.
- Ask parents to donate books or to help organize book drives.
- Apply for grants available through local, state, and national literacy organizations.

No matter where the books come from (within reason), make it clear at the beginning of the year that each student must come to reading workshop each day with enough reading material to last for at least thirty minutes. When the period begins they should have their books out and visible for you to check. Make this part of their participation grade. If a student comes to class without a book, deduct a certain number of points from his participation grade for the day. This works wonders. (The Participation Grade Sheet, a copy of which is provided in Appendix H, is discussed in greater detail later in the chapter.)

The time allotted to independent reading should not be eaten up with visits to the classroom library. Many teachers allow the first five or ten minutes for students to turn in and check out new books, especially for younger students, who are reading shorter books and finishing them more frequently. But older students, who are typically reading longer chapter books, may find this to-and-fro activity distracting. What works some years may not work others, and what works with one class may not work with another.

One year, too many of Jamie's students were shuffling around in the library looking for books at the beginning of independent reading, distracting those who were already reading. She and the students discussed the problem as a class (as all workshop concerns should be discussed) and came up with a solution they all agreed would work. They decided to make the classroom library available to students before school, during nutrition breaks, between classes, and after school. The students were then expected to come to class prepared to use all the time allotted to independent reading to read. Occasionally, a student would finish a book during class and need to return it and check out a new one. As long as the student signed the conference sheet and was quiet, he or she could go quickly and quietly to the classroom library to get a new book. The students also discovered that when they came in to check out a book outside of class, Jamie had time to help them select books that were just right for them.

Again, you and your students have to determine a library policy that works best for you, and you may need to revise it as issues or concerns arise. Be flexible, and include the entire class in discussing these concerns and making decisions. Jamie's students realized that since they had only one class period for language arts each day, they needed every minute of the workshop to read. And since she had made reading an expectation for these middle school students, they learned to handle that responsibility. They *can* handle responsibility! It all goes back to expectation.

Group Meeting Area

Workshops begin with a read-aloud or writing minilesson in the meeting area and end there as students share what they have read or written. It needs to be a place where students feel comfortable and know they are going to listen to and learn from one another as they discuss reading and writing. Most teachers put a large piece of soft carpet down on hard floors so students feel more comfortable sitting on the floor. Even on carpeted floors, we use an area rug to separate this area from the rest of our room. Often, local carpet or home-decorating stores will donate or at least discount a carpet if they know it is being used in a classroom. (Be sure to have the store print out fireproofing information in case your local fire codes require it.) Some teachers use smaller, individual carpets for younger students to sit on; some teachers find or make benches for older students. But we have never had a student complain about sitting on the floor!

Some teachers like to make the area even more comfortable by providing pillows, beanbag chairs, or upholstered chairs or couches, the privilege of using them earned by good behavior and participation. We've even asked for donations from parents in back-to-school letters and on back-to-school night. There are many parents out there looking for ways to help, especially parents of middle school students; they were used to being more involved in elementary school and want to continue to feel helpful.

Another thing you need in the meeting area is a read-aloud chair. This can be a regular desk chair, a cushioned chair, a rocking chair, a stool, or a bench. It just needs to be a comfortable place for reading aloud to the students and teaching minilessons. It is also a good idea to have a display surface for charts and notes, such as an easel with chart paper, a dry-erase board, or a chalkboard. It is also very helpful to have an overhead projector. With these things in place, you are ready for a year of reading aloud, presenting minilessons, and sharing.

Student Work Areas

Students need a quiet place with few distractions in which to read and write independently each day. Each student will of course have her or his own desk or seat at a table, but students should also be given the privilege of sitting or lying on the floor as long as they remain on task. Some students choose the meeting area as a good working place, while others choose little nooks and crannies in the room. We tell students to choose whatever place works best for them, and we closely monitor their work habits, especially in the beginning of the year. If a student does get off task, the privilege of choosing can be taken away temporarily and re-earned by following the workshop rules.

Conference Area

The conference area, sometimes a "conference corner," is the designated classroom area in which you can confer with individual readers and writers. This area may also be used for peer writing conferences. A small table with two chairs side by side works well, as long as you can still keep on eye on the rest of the class. There should also be a place for students to sign up for conferences. It could be a chalkboard, a dry-erase board, a laminated poster, or simply a piece of paper on a clipboard with a pen attached. See what works best for your students and your classroom layout. Forms that you and your students may use during reading or writing conferences should be readily available.

Anecdotal Records   We keep anecdotal notes for each student on index cards—one each for reading and writing—organized alphabetically by class and stored in separate boxes on the conference table. We jot down the date and a brief note about each conference we have with a student. Other teachers keep a notebook with a section for each student, using one notebook for reading and one for writing. These records document the skills or strategies you have taught and your students' strengths and weaknesses. You will use them to guide future instruction as well. We also keep the library cards of checked-out books at the conference table, as well as sticky notes for marking and annotating particular passages in books.

Student Reading Folder   Students bring their individual reading folder to each reading conference. (A manila folder, with the student's name and "Reading Folder" written on the tab, works best.) Students record what they read each day on the Daily Reading Log (see Appendix J), writing down the title, the author's name, and the number of the page on which they started reading. (At the end of the period, they record the number of the page on which they stopped reading.) This sheet documents everything the student reads in class all year and serves as a motivational tool since students chart their progress. It also helps the teacher determine instruction. Students record the name of each book completed on the Books I Have Read form (see Appendix I) after participating in a brief conference verifying that they have indeed completed the book. We staple the Daily Reading Log to the left side of the manila folder and the Books I Have Read form to the right side.

We introduce the reading folder and related forms in a minilesson at the beginning of the year. The folder becomes the cumulative record of what each student does in the classroom for the entire year, and we show it to parents during parent-teacher conferences.

Student Writing Folder   Students keep all information, notes, and handouts related to writing workshop, as well as drafts of their works in progress, in a writing folder. (These folders should have pockets.) One record in particular that is continually kept up to date is Pieces I Have Written (see Appendix K), which lists every piece of writing contained in the folder. It allows students (and the teacher) to see their accomplishments at a glance and reminds them about pieces of writing they may want to revisit later.

Another important writing folder record is Skills I Have Learned (Appendix L), an ongoing record that students add to as they learn new writing conventions during individual conferences, peer conferences, or minilessons. It can be used as a checklist while editing writing for publication. It can also be used to personalize the rubric for evaluating a final draft.

Materials Center

This is the area in which materials and supplies students will need during the workshop, particularly a writing workshop, are stored. Some teachers have a central chest or cart that students go to individually as needed; other teachers make separate supply kits for each table. Supplies that should be included are:

- various writing utensils: regular and colored pens and pencils, crayons, markers, highlighters, etc.
- lined and unlined paper for writing and illustrating
- pencil sharpener
- rulers
- staplers and staples
- glue
- scissors
- sticky notes
- paper clips

Also include any other supplies that will help the students as they write, particularly during the publishing stage when they design and create their own books. Some teachers even have a shelf or crate full of clipboards that students can use while writing. Make this area easily accessible, and clearly label the drawers or containers to indicate the supplies they contain.

It is also a good idea to place a crate in the materials center with extra handouts and forms (minilesson handouts, grading rubrics, peer conference forms, self-assessment forms, etc.). These include but are not limited to:

- Ideas for Book Projects (Appendix F)
- Books I Have Read (Appendix I)
- Daily Reading Log (Appendix J)

- Pieces I Have Written (Appendix K)
- Skills I Have Learned (Appendix L)

Jamie's materials center is typically a series of crates with pullout drawers that are placed on a deep bookshelf. Above the bookcase is a corkboard on which are posted various charts summarizing procedures, rules, and necessary supplies, as well as important reference information (such as editing marks). Charts like these can also be hung with clothespins on lines hung across the room or along the walls.

Some teachers include trays in the materials area in which students can submit their work, perhaps writing they would like to publish or have the teacher edit. There may also be a tray for the teacher to return work to the students. See what works for you and your students.

While some teachers make students responsible for bringing the necessary workshop materials (reading and writing folders, writing notebooks, etc.) to class each day, others allow students to store these materials in the classroom so they are not lost or forgotten at home. Crates labeled by class period or table can hold all these materials. Sometimes the crates can be left on top of tables instead of stored at the materials center.

Figure 9–5

We give students a manila folder to use as a reading folder and ask them to bring in a bradded folder (with inside pockets) to use as a writing folder. The brads secure three-hole-punched handouts and forms, and one of the pockets is designated for work in progress. Some teachers color-code student folders by period, which makes grading and organization easier. In that case, either the school or the teacher needs to provide the folders. (You can purchase them in bulk when they are on sale.) Students also provide their own writing notebooks—composition books that they will later decorate.

Teacher Space

All teachers need a place in the classroom to call their own, a place where they can store administrative files, records, and supplies, and where they feel comfortable planning and working before and after school. Some teachers prefer a desk, while others prefer a table. You also deserve a comfortable chair for working before and after school and during your planning period. Filing cabinets or drawers are great for storing class, school, and district information; workshop ideas and lessons; calendars for lesson planning; writing supplies; grade books; student progress folders; and more. (Student progress folders contain important information gathered throughout the year about each student, such as the Student Information Sheet, inventories, discipline documentation, and test data.)

Make this space a place where you can plan and work easily. However, as a workshop teacher, you won't be spending much time there during the day. You'll be constantly on your feet, moving among the students or conferring at the conference area to assess, instruct, and facilitate learning.

Computer Publishing Center

If possible, set up an area where students can type and print their writing on a computer. Get as many computers as you can (old ones are fine as long as they have a word-processing program). We know teachers who have asked for donations from parents or businesses and received them. A single printer can be hooked up to many computers, and all you really need is black ink.

If no computers are available, or if there is no room for them in your classroom, periodically take your students to the school computer lab. Learning how to type on a keyboard and use technology is an important part of most school, district, and state standards. This also makes the publishing process

Figure 9–6

much more exciting for your students, since they can revise more easily and create stories that look like real books (Figure 9–6).

These are only suggestions—things we've learned over the years that have worked for us and other teachers. No matter how you organize your classroom spaces, keep your focus on setting up classrooms that work for you and your students, keeping in mind those things that will help them become better readers and writers.

How Do I Organize the Schedule?

The most effective way to implement language arts is to schedule daily reading and writing workshops. Ideally, you want a large chunk of time each day for language arts, whether it be a ninety-minute block or two class periods back to back. That way you can use half the time for reading workshop and the other half for writing workshop. In too many schools language arts is squeezed into one forty-five-minute period a day, or else reading and writing are taught separately by different teachers, neither of which promotes optimum learning.

While you may be able to fight for a two-period block and win, many teachers have to struggle with one class period a day for language arts. If you find yourself in this situation, don't give up. The reading and writing workshop format can still work until you can convince those in charge to give you two periods.

We've seen teachers divide up the week between reading workshop and writing workshop; some spending Monday, Wednesday, and Friday on reading workshop and Tuesday and Thursday on writing workshop, then switch days the following week to balance the time spent on each. We've also seen some teachers spend Monday and Wednesday on reading workshop, Tuesday and Thursday on writing workshop, and then, on Friday, visit the school library to check out new books or the school computer lab to type stories. If that's your plan, sign up for library and computer lab visits as soon as possible.

Evaluate the amount of time you have, fight for more, and in the meantime, do what works best for you and your students. The most important thing is that the students are reading *and* writing all year long, since the two processes are so interconnected. Reading improves by reading. Writing improves by writing. And reading and writing improve each other.

Organization and structure are critical to the effectiveness of a workshop classroom. Being prepared each day is also critical. Only within a structured and organized classroom following a predictable schedule can students flourish as readers and writers. This kind of classroom will enable workshop to take on a life of its own.

What Do I Do the First Days of School?

The classroom is set up and organized, the students have arrived, and it's time to begin. This can be the most unnerving time of the year for both teachers and students. We are wondering who they are and what they're like, and they are just as curious about us. First impressions are inevitable and will determine how smoothly the first few weeks will go, so we must be prepared and ready to calm their nerves (as well as ours) and welcome them into our workshop classroom. The first days of workshop are critical in laying the foundation for what will happen the rest of the year.

Introducing the Workshop Schedule

Running a workshop classroom successfully depends on organization and consistency. We begin the first day of school by gathering the students in the meeting area to discuss, first of all, what reading and writing workshops are. Unfortunately, this is the first time most of our students have heard of this kind of classroom. We discuss what happens during reading and writing workshops, what the schedule looks like, and what the students will be expected to do every day. We project transparencies of the charts A Typical Schedule for Reading Workshop (see Chapter 1) and A Typical Schedule for Writing Workshop (see Chapter 5). We then post copies of these charts (or handwritten originals) on the walls of the classroom and follow that structure every day of the year, with the exception of library days, book project days, or author celebrations.

Establishing Rules and Procedures

Once students understand what reading and writing workshops are, we introduce the workshop rules and procedures. First, we lead a discussion of what it takes for a classroom to be successful. Students know what a successful class requires, and if they take part in establishing their own rules, they will be more likely to follow them. Together we come up with a list of rules, then post these rules in the classroom as a visual reminder, especially in the beginning of the year, of what is expected of the students every day.

Rules and their strict enforcement are critical to the success of a workshop classroom. We must have rules, and students must follow those rules. We make sure they know that they have lots of choices. They choose the books they read, the topics they write about, where they sit during independent reading and writing, and who they confer with, as long as they obey the class rules, but they do not get to choose whether they will obey the rules.

Making Participation a Part of Their Grade

On the overhead the first day of class, we project the Participation Grade Sheet (Appendix H) and explain that this is how their daily reading and writing grades will be determined. They automatically receive 100 points when they enter the classroom. It is up to them to keep those 100 points. If they listen when they are supposed to listen, read when they are supposed to read, and write when they are supposed to write, they will improve. It is their responsibility to follow the rules. It is our responsibility to make sure the rules are enforced, because we are responsible for our students' improvement. Since their participation will determine how much students improve, that participation should be and will be the source of their major grades in both reading and writing. There will be one participation grade each day for reading and one for writing. We go over the code at the bottom of the grade sheet:

- M—Materials
  - What materials must you have ready when *reading workshop* begins?
    Something to read
    Something to write with
    Reading folder
  - What materials must you have ready when *writing workshop* begins?
    Something to write with
    Writing notebook or folder (whichever you decide to use)
    Topic to write about

- O—Off task
  - What is considered off-task behavior during *independent reading*?
    Anything that is not related to reading. (We talk through several scenarios—"Is it okay to write during independent reading?" etc.)
  - What is considered off-task behavior in *independent writing*?
    Anything that is not related to writing. (We talk through several scenarios—"Is it okay to do homework during independent writing?" etc.)

- T—Talking
  - When is it appropriate to talk during *reading workshop*?
    Discussion before, during, and after a read-aloud
    Sharing at the end
    Conferences with the teacher
  - When is it appropriate to talk during *writing workshop*?
    Debriefing
    Sharing in small groups or as a class
    Peer conferences
    Teacher conferences

- ■ S—Out of seat
  - • When is it appropriate to be out of your seat during *reading workshop*?
    We talk through several scenarios—"Is it okay to get up and go to the trash can while I'm reading aloud to you?" "Is it okay to get up and go to the pencil sharpener during independent reading?" Students know they are not allowed to go to the classroom library to change books or get a new book without signing up for a teacher conference. Entering their name on the conference sheet allows them to go to the classroom library, get a book, and sit back down and read until we call them for a conference.
  - • When is it appropriate to be out of your seat during *writing workshop*? Again, we talk through several scenarios—"Is it okay to get up and go to the trashcan while I'm presenting a minilesson?" "Is it okay to get up and go to the pencil sharpener during the minilesson?"

You can personalize your marking system to meet the rules set up by the class. For example, you could mark a *D* for being disrespectful, since a prohibition against this usually finds its way onto most classroom rule lists. We also use the Participation Grade Sheet as a record of student attendance and tardiness by crossing through a box with a slash (/) if a student is absent or entering *TT* if a student is tardy. We keep these sheets on a clipboard, one sheet for each period, and this clipboard goes with us everywhere. If a student receives several warnings/deductions for poor behavior, there are specific consequences, which we record on the sheets as well. These sheets are filed in a special folder and become our documentation for student participation throughout the year.

This sheet has worked in our classrooms and in the classrooms of many teachers we've worked with, not only as a management tool but also as a basis for assigning grades. This is an authentic grading tool because it is based on the participation of the student. From day one we tell the students that it is our job to make sure that they are involved every minute of the class period, because that is the number one predictor of improvement—and this should be what grades demonstrate.

Making participation a part of the grade allows each student to be successful no matter how well he or she can read or write. As long as students are working and practicing, they can make good grades. This is a new opportunity for many struggling readers and writers who have never been able to make good grades in language arts. We've seen just this small change lift their motivation to read, write, and improve, because success breeds success.

Getting Started Checklist

Figure 9–7 is an example of a more detailed checklist you might use in making sure the classroom is prepared and organized before the first day of school arrives. It incorporates all of the things we've discussed in this chapter.

Design classroom layout with the following workshop areas

- Meeting area
- Carpet or rug
- Easel with chart paper, chalkboard, and/or dry-erase board
- Overhead projector
- Read-aloud chair
- Pillows, beanbag chairs, etc.
- Independent work area
- Desks or tables
- Library
- Books
- Bookshelves
- Baskets
- Conference area
- Student conference cards or forms
- Various quick tools for assessment
- Pens, pencils, sticky notes
- Conference sign-up spot
- Materials center
- Workshop supplies and forms
- Teacher space
- Desk or table and chair
- Filing cabinet for organizing school information, calendars, lessons, ideas, student progress folders, etc.
- Writing supplies
- Grade book/attendance records
- Computer publishing center
- Computer(s) with word processor softrware
- Printer with ink and paper
- CDs or disks to save student work

Create Library Management System

- Organize books on shelves and displays and in baskets
- Determine library rules and procedures for checking out and returning a book

Prepare introductory charts, such as

- Workshop Expectations
- Workshop Supplies Needed Daily
- Workshop Daily Schedule
- Library Rules
- Library Procedures

Make copies of introductory handouts, such as

- Participation Grade Sheets
- Classroom Guidelines
- Personal Interest Inventory
- Reading Survey
- Writing Survey
- Daily Reading Log
- Books I Have Read
- Pieces I Have Written
- Skills I Have Learned

Write students' names (from class lists) on

- Individual conference cards/forms
- Participation Grade Sheets for each class period

Figure 9–7 Getting Started Checklist

Go Right to the Source
Student Evaluations Show the Way

When we start to ask for our students' evaluations, they often surprise us, and we realize how far we might have gone astray without their insights. Their thoughts beget adjustments in our teaching and then we have to ask them, again, what they think. They evaluate. We revise what we do, and, eventually, we find ourselves in a teaching situation that can't exist without the frequent evaluations of students. We thirst for their insights.

—JANE HANSEN

It's amazing what your students will tell you if you give them the opportunity. And it's amazing how much we can learn from them if we take the time to listen. If you are ever in doubt about whether you're doing what's best for your students, let them tell you. Their words are your greatest assessment tool. Their strong voices give you the impetus to continue teaching what really matters.

As teachers today, we can easily let the weight and pressure of the job distract us from our readiness to share our thoughts, ideas, and love of reading and writing with our students. But our students can help ease that pressure and lighten our load if we let them. Over and over again, we find ourselves rejuvenated by what our students have to say when we allow them time to reflect on their individual learning and growth. During these self-assessments, roles reverse and weight shifts, as students remind us that they are indeed learning and growing as readers and writers—that we are indeed doing what's best for them.

Each time we read our students' personal reflections and evaluations, each time we are blown away by their thoughts, ideas, and energy, we are reminded of the impact the workshop classroom has on them and of the importance of allowing them time for ongoing self-reflection and self-evaluation in an environment that encourages these activities. Students are ready to share, and their reflections are full of insight and powerful messages for us, their teachers. Their words can inspire us, provide validation that we're doing what's best for them, offer further insight into their individual strengths and needs as readers and writers, and shed light on the roles we can play in their learning.

Their own reflections offer more insight into each student than any worksheet ever could. Self-assessment is an opportunity for students to exercise metacognitive skills as they evaluate their individual learning processes. It allows them to reflect on the quality of their work: *Did I do my best or could I do better? How can I improve the quality of my writing?* It allows teachers to see how students view themselves as learners and what their strengths and needs are. We can then use these reflections to guide and differentiate instruction, whether whole group, small group, or individualized, to meet their needs. It all depends on who needs what, when. This kind of instruction is much more meaningful, since our students have identified these needs themselves—and thus created a greater purpose for learning—and have an authentic way to implement what is learned in their own writing. And yes, they can do this.

If you show them what good writing looks and sounds like, continuously engage them in conversation about the qualities of good writing, and teach them various strategies that good writers use, they will be able to read their own writing and point out its strengths and weaknesses. Once they are invested in their own stories, they will feel more comfortable and confident telling you what they still need to do and learn in order to make it better. Because the work is theirs, they care and want to learn how to improve it. Don't underestimate your students' intelligence and ability to be engaged and active in their learning. Just provide a literate environment in which to learn, one in which you are always reading, writing, discussing, and discovering together, one in which they are respected and feel safe to learn, to share, and to receive meaningful responses from you and their classmates.

This isn't something we do only as writers. Self-assessment is woven into every aspect of learning. We are constantly evaluating and discussing our accomplishments, allowing the process to push us toward even higher goals. Of course, much of this discussion takes place in conferences, but it is also important to keep written records of our growth. Having the opportunity to write about their learning encourages students to think more deeply about who they are as learners.

Have your students keep a list of personal reading goals and allow them to reflect on what they can do to achieve them, how they are doing along the way, and what it feels like once they get there. Ask them to write about how they feel as readers, what they are interested in reading, what books they hear are good, what authors or genres they would like to try out, and so forth. These pieces of information paint a picture of what you can do to help each student become a lifelong reader.

Throughout the year, we ask our students to reflect on various aspects of our reading and writing workshops: what they've learned, what or who has helped them learn and grow, and what could help them grow even more. These reflections often reveal the value students place on various workshop components, such as the read-aloud or time spent reading or writing independently, and we are always curious about how we can make our workshops meet their needs even better, to make the school year even more successful.

Even more important than what we get out of student self-assessments is what the students get out of it. Here's just one example. Throughout the year, Jamie's sixth graders had become used to assessing themselves by answering questions she provided as a handout or projected on the overhead. At the end of the year, Jamie decided to make it more personal. She asked students to write her an informal, conversational letter (Figure 10–1).

Troy had entered Jamie's classroom about a month into the school year, after he'd been dropped from the district's gifted and talented program. Naturally, he arrived thinking he was stupid. Socially he was different from his peers. He had read so many books and was so intelligent that his language sounded different, and he was misunderstood by his classmates. But Troy was a truly gifted writer, and Jamie's reading and writing workshops allowed that ability to shine and gave other students a way to understand him and respect him for his talent.

Even though Troy was a talented writer, it was hard for him to get his ideas down on paper at the beginning of the year. Trying to do so paralyzed him. It was as if he had so much in his head, he couldn't figure out where to begin. But with time and encouragement and everything else that is part of a workshop classroom, he was finally able to break through this barrier. Troy's

Letter Requirements

- Place the completed letter in the front pocket of your portfolio.

- Must be typed or neatly handwritten on front side of paper only.

- Must be in letter format, including: date, salutation (e.g., Dear Ms. Marsh), and closing (e.g., Sincerely, *Your Name*).

- Must be edited for spelling and grammatical errors.

- Must be organized in paragraphs.

Letter Content

- After compiling, organizing, and analyzing your portfolio contents, write me a letter in which you reflect on this English class by addressing all of the following points, in your order of preference:

  - How do you think you have changed as a reader this school year? How have you changed as a writer this school year? (This may include interest, attitude, and academic growth.)

  - In your opinion, what or who has caused this change? (Please provide specific examples.)

  - What do you think about the way this language arts class was set up as a reading-writing workshop? How do you think you benefited as a reader and writer and as an individual from being in this workshop classroom?

  - What was your favorite part of the reading-writing workshop? Why?

  - What are your future goals as a reader and writer? This may include short-term goals as well as long-term goals.

  - How will what you've learned as a reader and writer influence your future? How will it play a part in what you want to be or accomplish in life?

  - Please share with me any other thoughts, ideas, or reflections you have about yourself, me as your teacher, this class, reading, writing, or life in general. This is your chance to share with me anything you would like before moving on.

- Please be as specific and detailed as possible in your writing. Provide me with a full explanation of your thoughts and ideas.

I am looking forward to reading your letters!

Figure 10–1 Letter to Ms. Marsh

letter to Jamie at the end of the year is more revealing than any exam could ever be:

Dear Ms. Marsh,

Thank you for a year of growth and learning. Although I still struggle at times to put my thoughts down on paper, this is the first time in my life I have felt confident that I can put all of my thoughts onto paper, even if it takes time. It used to be that I'd only put down in writing what I thought other people wanted. I ended up spending too much time thinking about it. Now, I just put onto paper what I feel like and I don't think too much about it. This year I've also been able to connect with stories better and enter into the characters, making my reading more enjoyable.

My growth this year as a reader and writer is due to many reasons. Some growth came from family. For example, drawings by my brother, Kyle, inspired me to create a certain style of characters in my stories. A few anime television shows have given me ideas for settings and certain items of interest in my stories. I never have truly been able to have freedom in my writing, because in most writing projects they SAY that you have freedom, but they always give you guidelines that restrict good ideas from getting on paper. In your class, however, there were little to no restrictions on the writing assignments. This helped me to get my own stories down on paper. For example, I've had ideas for every genre, but when the teachers in the past have put so many restrictions on the assignment, the ideas I have no longer fit.

I think the workshop set-up of the class was great. It let the students work at their own pace and it put little to no stress on the student for unreasonable deadlines. My favorite part of the reading-writing workshop was doing the book projects. I liked how much freedom we had to do whatever we wanted with the project. I enjoyed being able to share books that I liked, but that most people wouldn't read. It gave me a chance to do something FOR the book. If the book fascinated me, then I felt like I had a chance to give something back to the book by sharing it and give the other students a chance to enjoy the book too.

As a writer, I want to be able to perfect my ideas a little bit better before I put them on paper. I do want to be a writer and publish a book, and in a sense, throwing a chunk of my ideas and thoughts into the great cosmos of other writers' creations and see how their ideas compare to mine. As a reader, the only thing I really know that I want to get better at is remembering characters names a little better and getting less obsessed over sequels to my favorite books.

I think my skills as a reader will help me gain ideas and thoughts to help me make things I write and say original. Being a good reader helps me to have a deeper understanding of many things. My skills as a writer will help me be a better communicator and to be understood and appreciated better and make me more approachable. It will also allow me to show people that I am a smart person.

Mrs. Marsh, you are a wonderful teacher. You allow your students to express their true selves with creativity better than any teacher I have had. It would be a shame for you to ever stop teaching because I would like to imagine one day seeing one of your students doing a book project on one of the books me or one of your other students (now) will have created. Wouldn't that be cool!

Sincerely,
Troy

If we are supposed to be here to facilitate our students' learning, then we must allow them to be actively engaged in the process, reflecting on who they are, where they are, what they know, where they want to go, and what knowledge and skills they still need to get there. We must give them the opportunity to invite us on their journeys as they share their thoughts with us. This means that we need to give them the time and opportunity to reflect on their individual growth and then really listen to what they have to say, allowing it to penetrate into the core of our instruction and guide us through a process of learning together.

On Endings and Beginnings

D ay after day, as we work in the *real* world in *real* classrooms with *real* students, we are reminded of the *real* purpose of education. It's not passing yet another test. It's not grades. It's not paperwork and competition. It's not homework or benchmarks or report cards or scope-and-sequence charts or the next meeting to plan the next meeting. Even though these things are part of our reality as teachers, our purpose is to find our way into the complex lives of each and every student we have stewardship over. The statement "A child doesn't care how much we know until he knows how much we care" gets to the heart of the matter. We have to first find our way in—then and only then will our students be ready to learn.

Reading and writing and caring are our way in.

One of the first things we are taught to do when writing anything, whether it is an article, a short story, a poem, or a book like this one, is to immerse ourselves in that kind of writing. By doing so, we familiarize ourselves with the structure and voice of writers of that genre. Fletcher and Portalupi (1998) state, "We can often tell which students are avid readers because their writing has the sound of book language. In search for their own writers' voices, students will try on the style of the writers they love and admire." (p. 77) This is a powerful lesson. Reading and writing go hand in hand. Authors are continuously influenced by the stories that surround them. Nancie Atwell (1987) writes:

> Students who seldom read for pleasure, seldom choose their own books, or seldom encounter texts that capture their imaginations or satisfy their needs, will not become literary borrowers. Elementary school students who read only the voiceless committee prose of basals don't borrow, nor do secondary school students who read the prescribed canon of anthologized classics. It is what captivates students as readers that inspires writing. (p. 241)

We have seen firsthand, as writers and as teachers of writing who hear and read our students' stories, just how much our favorite authors impact our writing and teach us how to write. If our students are not exposed to these voices, they may never find their own voice and develop their own craft as writers. "When we explore conditions that allow students to learn about the writer's craft, we cannot leave out the presence of literature: stories, songs, poems, and books. This may be the most crucial condition of all. The writing you get out of your students can only be as good as the classroom literature that surrounds and sustains it" (Fletcher and Portalupi 1998, p. 10).

The best writing teachers our students have are the authors of the books they are reading. Every day when we walk into our writing workshops faced with the challenge of helping our students develop as writers, we feel calmer and more confident in the knowledge that we don't have to do it alone. As long as our students remain immersed in real books with stories they connect to and enjoy and are given the opportunity to practice and develop their own craft as writers, the authors of those books join us in facilitating the emergence of better writers. Professionals are standing by.

But students must also be surrounded by one another's stories. As they share together every day, they immerse themselves in one another's voices, further inspiring each other as writers. Atwell (1987) states:

> There is no more important source of inspiration for writers in the workshop than other writers' pieces, no single more important kind of reading. When the context is right—when kids can choose their own topics and share what they've written—other students respond to the authentic voices and information by borrowing what captivates them to create voice and information of their own. (p. 249)

When students feel safe reading, writing, and sharing in an environment in which they are not judged, an environment in which everyone is embarking on the process of writing, an environment in which students inspire one another and grow together, then walls are lifted, barriers are broken, and students are capable of so much more than we can imagine. Writing no longer is something done just to pass a standardized test. It is not formulaic. It is not prescribed. It is not artificial. Writing becomes very powerful, very personal, even cathartic.

For many students, writing becomes one of their only ways to sort through life's problems and come to realizations. They enter our classrooms year after year with real issues, issues that take precedence over anything we ask them to do in school. We cannot ignore this. We must accept who they are. We must respect where they come from. We must acknowledge them as individuals with valuable life experiences and knowledge. We must create a safe and encouraging environment that allows them to feel comfortable enough to open up and let us in.

Our purpose as teachers is not so much about *teaching* as it is about *reaching* and *caring*. Our students will learn when and if they have a passion to learn. For too many of our older students, that passion has been extinguished. Finding and nurturing these passions in our kids, lighting the fire within each one of them and then fanning the flame to keep it going—*that's* our job as a teacher. And what better way to do it than by creating reading and writing classrooms where this can happen—where our students can discover those passions within and where we have the time to build those caring, trusting relationships so we can help them find them. It's about establishing environments where students feel free to take risks—where they can open up and invite us in.

What we've outlined in this book works with all kids, because it gets to the heart of teaching: caring. Life does go on. Tests and grades and report cards come and go. But that doesn't have to be our focus. Success breeds success, so we need to find ways to help students feel successful and be successful. If we set up workshop classrooms in which students can find that place of belonging—the knowledge that someone cares—then perhaps they'll trust us enough to let us in. Then and only then will they be ready to learn so that we *can* teach them.

This is the end of this book, but it is the beginning of more stories to tell. There are more stories waiting to be discovered, more life issues waiting to be dealt with. The form—memoir, fiction, nonfiction, poetry—doesn't matter. As Rachel says in *Summer of Fear*, "For too long now I have dwelt upon the past. It is a time now for new beginnings." Through their reading and their writing, with our support, students can find their new beginnings. As can we.

Appendix A Student Information Sheet

Student Name _____ Home Phone _____

Birth Date _____ Elementary _____

Home Address _____

_____

CONTACT INFORMATION:

MOTHER/Guardian Name _____

Home Phone _____ Work Phone _____

Cell Phone _____ Pager _____

Home Address _____

_____

Email Address _____

FATHER/Guardian Name _____

Home Phone _____ Work Phone _____

Cell Phone _____ Pager _____

Home Address _____

_____

Email Address _____

Please circle the following things your child has access to at home:

COMPUTER   PRINTER   EMAIL   INTERNET

Student's Interest/Strengths _____

_____

_____

_____

Is there any other information I should know, including medical issues? _____

_____

_____

_____

© 2007 by Linda Ellis and Jamie Marsh from *Getting Started*. Portsmouth, NH: Heinemann.

Appendix B   Reading Survey by Nancie Atwell

Name _____ Date _____

1. If you had to guess . . .

   How many books would you say you owned? _____

   How many books would you say there are in your house? _____

   How many books would you say you've read since school let out in May? _____

   How many books would you say you read during the last school year, September to May? _____

   And how many of those books did you choose for yourself? _____

2. What are the best three books you've ever read, or had read aloud to you?

   _____

   _____

   _____

3. In your ideal novel, what would the main character be like?

   _____

   _____

   _____

4. What are your favorite genres—or kinds—of books to read?

   _____

   _____

   _____

5. Who are your favorite authors these days? List as many as you'd like.

   _____

   _____

   _____

6. Which poets are your favorites?

   _____

   _____

   _____

continued on next page

7. What are some of the ways you decide whether you'll read a book?

   _____

   _____

   _____

8. Have you ever liked a book so much that you reread it? _____ If so, can you name it/some of them here?

   _____

   _____

   _____

9. What do you think someone has to know or do in order to be a strong, happy reader of books? List as many abilities, attitudes, approaches, and kinds of knowledge as you can think of.

   _____

   _____

   _____

10. What do you think are your own three greatest strengths as a reader of books?

    _____

    _____

    _____

11. What would you like to get better at as a reader of books? List at least three of your current goals.

    _____

    _____

    _____

12. Do you know the title(s) of the book(s) you'd like to read next? _____ If so, please tell me.

    _____

    _____

    _____

13. In general, how do you feel about reading, and about yourself as a reader?

    _____

    _____

    _____

Adapted from In the Middle *by Nancie Atwell. Copyright 2006 by Nancie Atwell. Published by Heinemann, a division of Reed Elsevier, Inc., Portsmouth, NH. Used by permission.*

Appendix C   Personal Interest Inventory

The goal of these questions is to find out some of the things you do and how you feel about certain things. Please answer each question truthfully and carefully.

1. Do you like to read? Check one answer:

    a little _____   a lot _____   an average amount _____   not at all _____

2. How many comic books do you read every week? _____

3. What are your favorite comic strips in the newspaper?

    1. _____   2. _____   3. _____

4. Do you take a newspaper at your house? _____ Which one? _____

    How often do you read a newspaper? Check one answer:

    Daily _____   Sundays _____   Once in a while _____   Never _____

    Which section do you read first? _____

    How much time do you spend reading a daily newspaper? _____

5. Which magazines do you like to read?

    1. _____   2. _____

    3. _____   4. _____

6. Which magazines do you read regularly?

    1. _____   2. _____

    3. _____   4. _____

    What do you like about these magazines? _____

7. When did you last read a book not assigned for a class? Date: _____

8. Name the three best books you ever read.

    1. Title & Author: _____

    2. Title & Author: _____

    3. Title & Author: _____

9. If you could buy as many books as you wanted, what would they be? _____

    _____

    _____

    _____

continued on next page

10. What kinds of books do you like? Place an L in front of each type of book that you like. Place an N in front of each type of book that you do not like.

___traditional	___modern realistic fiction	___poetry
___fantasy	___science fiction	___biography
___informational	___love stories	___mythology
___baseball	___true life adventures	___movie stars
___criminals	___comics	___essays
___war stories	___football	___nature stories
___mysteries	___basketball	___dictionaries
___famous people	___horses	___space travel
___mathematics	___cowboy stories	___encyclopedias
___how to make things	___teenage problems	___politics
___trivia	___travel articles	___science

11. What do teenagers read about?_____

_____

12. If you wanted to write a book, what would the title be? _____

_____

13. What books have you read that you disliked very much? Why?

_____

_____

14. Name the three living men you admire the most:

1._____ 2._____ 3._____

Name the three living women you admire the most:

1._____ 2._____ 3._____

Who are your favorite heroes from the past? _____

15. What hobbies or collections do you have? _____

16. What things do you like to do most in your spare time?

1._____ 2._____

3._____ 4._____

17. What are your favorite television programs?

1._____ 2._____

3._____ 4._____

continued on next page

18. Do you listen to the radio? _____ Name the stations: _____

19. Name your four favorite movies:

    1. _____   2. _____

    3. _____   4. _____

20. List the stage plays you have seen.

    1. _____   2. _____

21. Who are your favorite entertainers?

    1. _____   2. _____

    3. _____   4. _____

22. To which clubs or organizations do you belong?

    _____

    _____

23. Do you take any kind of special lessons after school? If so, what kind? Do you enjoy that
    activity? _____

24. Do you enjoy sports? Which sports do you enjoy most?

    1. _____   2. _____

    Do you have a favorite team? _____   Name of team _____

    Do you have a favorite player? _____   Name of player _____

25. Where is your favorite place to visit? Favorite vacation spot?

    _____

    _____

    If you could take a trip anywhere in the world, where would you go? Why?

    _____

26. What do you want to be when you finish school? _____

    What do your parents want you to be? _____

27. Suppose you had three wishes that might come true. Name your wishes:

    1. _____

    2. _____

    3. _____

28. Of all the things you do in school, which do you like best? _____

    _____

Appendix D   The Burke Reading Interview
Modified for Older Readers

1. When you are reading and you come to something that gives you trouble, what do you do? Do you ever do anything else?

2. Who is a good reader you know?

3. What makes _____ a good reader?

4. Do you think _____ ever comes to something that gives him/her trouble when he/she is reading?

5. When _____ does come to something that gives him/her trouble, what do you think he/she does about it?

6. How would you help someone who was having difficulty reading?

7. What would a teacher do to help that person?

8. How did you learn to read?

9. Is there anything you would like to change about your reading?

10. Describe yourself as a reader: What kind of reader are you?

11. What do you read routinely, like every day or every week?

12. What do you like most of all to read?

13. Can you remember any special book or the most memorable thing you have ever read?

14. What is the most difficult thing you have to read?

Adapted from *Reading Miscue Inventory* by Y. Goodman, D. Watson, and C. Burke. Copyright © 2005 by Y. Goodman, D. Watson, and C. Burke. Reprinted by permission of Richard C. Owen Publishers, Inc.

Appendix E   Instructions for Miscue Analysis

1. After administering the Personal Interest Inventory and Burke Reading Interview Modified for Older Readers, tape-record the student reading an entire story without assistance and then a retelling of as much of the story as he remembers. Code the story as follows:

   ✔ Substitutions—Mary ~~ran~~ to the store. *(rode)*

   ✔ Non-word Substitutions—Mary ~~ran~~ to the store. *(rin)*

   ✔ Partial-word Substitutions—Mary ran to the ~~store~~. *(st)*

   ✔ Dialect—Mary ran to the ~~store~~. *(sto)*

   ✔ Omissions—Jose could ~~not~~ come to the party.

   ✔ Insertions—Shameka ran across the grass and ∧ fell into the puddle. *(she)*

   ✔ Reversals—Can they go?

   ✔ Repetitions

      • Correcting a miscue—Collin could not ~~come~~ with us. *(go) ©*

      • Abandoning a correct form—She went along with the other girls. *(alone) (ac)*

      • Unsuccessful attempt—He ran down the sidewalk. *(uc) ① sid ② sidwa ③ sidwak ④ sidwalk*

      • Plain repetition—Ana <u>ate an apple</u>.

2. Transfer 25 miscues to a Miscue Summary Sheet as follows:

   • Don't record miscues from the first paragraph.

   • Don't record a miscue more than once.

   • Don't record proper names.

   • Don't record miscues the student self corrected.

Reader/Text	Graphic Similarity	Sound Similarity	Syntactic Acceptability	Semantic Acceptability
rode/ran	—	—	✓	—
rin/ran	✓	✓	✓	—
st/store	—	✓	—	—
—/not	—	—	✓	—
she/—	—	—	✓	✓
sid/sidwa/sidwak/sidwalk	✓	✓	✓	—

continued on next page

Miscue Summary Sheet

Reader _____ Grade Level _____ Self-Correction Rate _____ %

Name of Selection _____ Reading Level _____

Reader/Text (What the reader said/ what is in the text)	Graphic Similarity (Are half or more of the letters the same?)	Sound Similarity (Are half or more of the sounds the same?)	Syntactic Acceptability (Does the substitution sound like language?)	Semantic Acceptability (Is the meaning of the sentence preserved?)
Total				
Percentage (Total divided by 25)				

continued on next page

3. Analyze the miscues using the following as a guide:

- Graphophonic—Is the reader using knowledge of letters and sounds?

  – Graphic Similarity? Does the substitution *look* like the text word?
  – Are half or more letters the same? (e.g., pretty for party)
  – Sound Similarity? Does the substitution *sound* like the text word?
  – Are half or more the sounds the same? (e.g., sound for round)

- Syntactic—Within the context of the sentence, does the substitution sound like language?

  a. Substituting noun for noun, verb for verb, etc. (e.g., daddy for dad)
  b. Using a nonword with an inflected ending (e.g., dunted for darted)
  c. Making the sentence sound grammatically sensible even though it may not be meaningful.

	pripping
Example:	The cat is playing on the grass.

- Semantic Acceptability—Is the meaning preserved?

  Does the substitution make sense within the context of the sentence and the passage? If the student is using meaning as a cue to reading, the error will reveal substitutions that are close to the thought of the sentence and that do not change the idea of the story.

	little
Example:	The small girl is pretty.

Scoring—Reading patterns are determined by calculating the percentages of each substitution category. For example, if 8 of 25 are graphically similar, the percentage is 32% (i.e., the student is using graphic information 32% of the time). Do not record the self-corrections on the analysis sheet but get a self-correction rate by counting the total number of self-corrections and dividing by the total number of miscues including the self-corrections (i.e., 15 self-corrections out of a total of 30 miscues (including the self-corrections) is a 50% self-correction rate. This can be an important signal that the reader is on his way to success. Successful readers use all three cueing systems simultaneously. If he is self-correcting, he is using all three cueing systems.

Adapted from *Reading Miscue Inventory* by Y. Goodman, D. Watson, and C. Burke. Copyright © 2005 by Y. Goodman, D. Watson, and C. Burke. Reprinted by permission of Richard C. Owen Publishers, Inc.

Appendix F Ideas for Book Projects

Writing

___ 1. Write the story in a book from a different point of view. Take an entire story (or part of it) and write a version as someone else would tell it. (For example, the third pig in *The Three Little Pigs* might say, "I told my brothers that straw and sticks just wouldn't do. Those are no protection from a hungry wolf. Now me, I'm using bricks!")

___ 2. Write the diary a main character might have written. Imagine you are the person in your book. Write a diary for a few days or weeks as he or she would have done.

___ 3. Write a character sketch of someone in a book. This might be the central character or a minor supporting character in the story. Tell what he looked like but also include favorite color, horoscope sign, sports liked, and even a car bumper sticker or a T-shirt.

___ 4. Rearrange a passage as a "found" poem. Find a particularly effective description or bit of action that is really poetry written as prose. Rewrite it. Leave out words or skip a sentence or two, but rearrange it to create a poem.

___ 5. Write a parody of a book. This kind of humorous imitation appeals to children. Parody the entire book or one scene.

___ 6. Write a promotion campaign for a movie about a book. This could include newspaper and layouts, radio and television commercials, and any special events.

___ 7. Write a letter to the author of a book. While authors may not have time to respond to each letter they receive (they might not get their next book done if they did), they do enjoy letters from their readers—especially those that discuss the book on children's own terms. Send letters in care of book publishers if you can't locate the author's address in *Who's Who, Current Biography*, or other reference sources. Include an addressed envelope and stamp with the letter.

___ 8. Put together a cast for the film version of a book. Imagine the director-producer wants a casting director to make recommendations. Decide who would be the actors and actresses. Include photos and descriptions of the stars and tell why each is "perfect" for the part. Write a report to convince the producer of the selections.

___ 9. Write a report of related information about one topic or person in a book. For example, research information about the trial of Benedict Arnold, how the covered wagons traveled, fishing off a particular island, and so on.

___ 10. Make a new book jacket. It should include an attractive picture or cover design, a summary of the book, information on the author and illustrator, and information about other books by that author.

___ 11. Convert a book to a radio drama. Give a live or taped version of the story—or a scene from it—as a radio play. Include an announcer and sound effects.

___ 12. Convert the events of a story into a ballad or song. Write the lyrics and music or adapt words to a melody by someone else.

continued on next page

Drama

_____ 13. Do a dramatic reading of a scene (readers theater). Select the scene and ask friends to help read it dramatically.

_____ 14. Convert a book into a puppet show. Make simple puppets (stick puppets, finger puppets, paper bag puppets, and so on), and present the story or an exciting scene from it.

_____ 15. Read a scene with special effects. Choose a particularly interesting passage and read it with a musical background or sound effects.

_____ 16. Do a "You are There" news program reporting on a particular scene, character, or event in a book.

_____ 17. Pretend you are a talk show host (e.g., Oprah Winfrey) and interview a character from your book or the author of your book.

_____ 18. Write and stage a television series episode. Think of a popular television series that a book or part of it would fit. Then convert it to that series and perform a segment before the class.

_____ 19. Do a takeoff on the old television program "This is Your Life," where the characters come to life. Role-play a character. The announcer describes important people in the life of the person honored. (This is especially suitable for biography or historical fiction, but could be adapted for any book.)

_____ 20. Prepare a television commercial about a book. Imagine a book is the basis for a miniseries on television. Prepare and give the television commercials that would make people watch it.

_____ 21. Use body masks and present a scene from your book. Make full-sized cardboard figures with cutouts for the face and hands. Use these to dramatize a scene.

_____ 22. Dramatize a scene from a book with other children taking parts. If desired, use props and costumes. If children know the story, improvise the scripts.

_____ 23. Play charades based on various books that members of the class have read. Review standard charade signals. Divide into teams. Then have children draw titles of books or the names of characters in books, concentrating on those that have been popular.

Art/Media

_____ 24. Make a soap or paraffin carving about an event or person in a book. These are inexpensive materials and soft, so there is little danger from tools used for carving.

_____ 25. Mold plaster relief designs. Pour plaster into a form over various objects and then antique or shellac them to make interesting displays about subjects in a book.

_____ 26. Make life-sized paper-stuffed animals, people, or objects found in a book. Cut out two large sheets of wrapping paper in the shape desired. Staple the edges almost all the way around. Stuff with crumpled newspaper, finish stapling, and paint.

continued on next page

____ 27. Make hand looms and weavings that portray a design in a book. Almost anything—from paper plates to forked sticks—will make a loom when strung with yarn, rope, or cord. Check arts and craft books for directions. Then use the creations as wall hangings or mobiles.

____ 28. Create batik designs with wax and old sheets of tie-dye material. When dry and ironed, use them for wall hangings, curtains, and costumes.

____ 29. Fashion a mobile from items related to a story. The mobiles add color and movement to a room. They could be displayed in the classroom, library, or cafeteria.

____ 30. Make a "roll-movie" of the scenes or events of a book. Put a series of pictures in sequence on a long strip of paper. Attach ends to rollers and place in a cardboard box. Print simple dialogue to accompany the frames.

____ 31. Create an animation of a scene on adding-machine tape. To make the animation, draw a sequence of pictures with each one showing a bit more movement than the preceding one. When this is rolled quickly (on a dowel, stick, or paper towel tube), it gives the appearance of motion.

____ 32. Create filmstrips of a story. Commercially produced material is available with special color pens to make filmstrips.

____ 33. Construct a diorama of a scene from a book. Old shoe boxes are a good size for making diorama scenes that can be simple or complicated.

____ 34. Print a design from a story in a book using a variety of materials. Here too, the process may be simple or complicated. Use potatoes or other raw vegetables to carve and use. Or try plastic meat trays and silk-screen prints.

____ 35. Use a collage to represent the mood of a book or its theme with words, colors, and pictures. Collages, popular and interesting to make, can frequently reveal a message in the book.

____ 36. Draw a scale model of an item in a story. Making an object from the story to scale presents many challenges. For example, try a go-cart, a matchlock gun, or any other item.

____ 37. Cook a food mentioned in your book. It's always fun to share something to eat. Make sure if you are going to share that there is enough for everyone in the class. Cook your recipe at school or home. Don't forget to practice safety!

____ 38. Build a relief map of the setting of a story. Use clay, sand, or papier-mâché.

____ 39. Design and make your own T-shirt of an illustration about a book. Create a design using colorfast markers, fabric paints, or computer printout appliqués.

____ 40. Construct a building or an item from a story you have read.

____ 41. Make some costume dolls for a display of characters in a book. Create costume dolls and display them.

____ 42. Complete scale drawings of rooms in a book. Use graph paper with a set scale, and design places portrayed in a book.

continued on next page

___ 43. Learn to play a game mentioned in a book. Use graph paper with a set scale, and design places portrayed in a book.

___ 44. Build a model of a scene or room in a story to scale with a taped description. This may be something accurately described in the book or an invention of what it should be like. Tape-record a description.

___ 45. Ask others in the class to design and stitch a square for a quilt. Depict favorite characters or scenes. Then stitch the quilt together. The individual squares may be drawn with marking pens or done in stitchery. The quilt may be a wall hanging, a curtain for a private reading area in the room, or presented to the school as a class gift.

Oral

___ 46. Impersonate a character and tell an episode in a book. Dress up as a character and retell the story.

___ 47. Interview a character from a book. Prepare questions to give to another student. The reader assumes the role of the character in the book and answers the questions as that character would.

___ 48. Conduct a small-group discussion. Several students who have read a particular book get together to discuss it.

___ 49. Focus a discussion about a particular person. Compare biographies of characters in historical fiction.

___ 50. Compare versions of the same story. Contrast different versions of one story or several stories with similar themes.

___ 51. Have a panel or round-table discussion of books on the same topic. Use one of the bibliographies of books on a particular topic (death, loneliness, disabilitites, heroes, heroines, and so on). Have the group present summaries of their books.

___ 52. Pitch a sales talk for a book. Give everyone in the class tokens, play money, or straw votes. After the sales talk, take bids to get the most for it.

___ 53. Interview a book's author. The reader becomes the author and comes to visit the class, who in turn interviews him or her.

___ 54. Portray a book character. Ask another reader of the same book to role-play a different character. The two characters can meet, talk about themselves, and discuss what has happened to them. This is especially appropriate if they have something in common: a similar adventure, similar jobs, and so on.

___ 55. Make a talking display of a book. Tape a dialogue or description about an event, scene, or character.

___ 56. Research the author's life and find other books written by him or her. Share this information with the class. You may even want to act as the author or include some visual aids to help illustrate the author's life.

Appendix G   Writing Survey by Nancie Atwell

Name _____   Date _____

1. Are you a writer? _____

    (If your answer is YES, then answer question 2a. If your answer is NO, answer 2b.)

2a. How did you learn to write?

    _____

    _____

or

2b. How do others learn to write?

    _____

    _____

3. What does someone have to do or know, in order to write well? List as many different abili-
    ties, kinds of knowledge, approaches, and ways of perceiving as you can think of.

    _____

    _____

4. What are your favorite genres to write?

    _____

    _____

5. What kinds of responses help you the most, in improving your writing and growing as a writer?

    _____

    _____

6. What are your three greatest strengths as a writer? (List them.)

    _____

    _____

7. What do you need to get better at as a writer? (List at least three of your goals, unrelated to
    handwriting.)?

    _____

    _____

8. What's the best thing that ever happened to you as a writer or because of your writing?

    _____

    _____

9. In general, how do you feel about writing and about yourself as a writer?

    _____

    _____

Adapted from *In the Middle* by Nancie Atwell. Copyright 2006 by Nancie Atwell. Published by Heinemann, a division of Reed Elsevier, Inc., Portsmouth, NH. Used by permission.

Appendix H   Participation Grade Sheet

Dates _____ Week _____ Period _____

	Student	M	T	W	R	F	Average
1							
2							
3							
4							
5							
6							
7							
8							
9							
10							
11							
12							
13							
14							
15							
16							
17							
18							
19							
20							
21							
22							
23							
24							
25							
26							
27							
28							
29							
30							

M—Materials (-30) O—Off Task (-10) T—Talking (-10) S—Out of Seat (-10) TT—Tardy (-10)

Appendix 1   Books I Have Read

Date	Title of Book	Author	Genre	Comment

T—Traditional   MRF—Modern Realistic Fiction   P—Poetry   SF—Science Fiction
F—Fantasy   HF—Historical Fiction   B—Biography   I—Informational

Appendix J   Daily Reading Log

Date	Title of Book	Author	Pg. Start	Pg. End

Appendix K   Pieces 1 Have Written

#	Title	Genre	Date Completed

Appendix L   Skills 1 Have Learned

Date	Skill

Works Cited

Abrahamson, Richard. 1987. Ten Commandments of a Good Reading Teacher. Paper read at Sam Houston Area Reading Council Conference, Huntsville, Texas.

Allington, Richard L. 1994. "The Schools We Have. The Schools We Need." *The Reading Teacher* 48 (September): 14–29.

———. 2001. *What Really Matters for Struggling Readers: Designing Research-based Programs.* New York, NY: Addison-Wesley.

———. 2002. "What I've Learned About Effective Reading Instruction from a Decade of Studying Exemplary Elementary Classroom Teachers." *Phi Delta Kappan* 83 (June): 740–47.

———. 2004. "Setting the Record Straight." *Educational Leadership* 61 (March): 22–25.

Anderson, Richard C., E. Heibert, J. Scott, and I. Wilkinson. 1985. *Becoming a Nation of Readers: The Report of the Commission on Reading.* Washington DC: National Institute of Education.

Anderson, Richard C., Paul T. Wilson, and Linda G. Fielding. 1988. "Growth in Reading and How Children Spend Their Time Outside of School." *Reading Research Quarterly* 23 (Summer): 285–303.

Atwell, Nancie. 1987. *In the Middle: Writing, Reading, and Learning with Adolescents.* Portsmouth, NH: Heinemann.

———. 1998. *In the Middle: New Understandings About Writing, Reading, and Learning.* Portsmouth, NH: Heinemann.

———. 2002. *Lessons That Change Writers.* Portsmouth, NH: Heinemann.

Bloom, Benjamin S., Max D. Engelhart, Edward J. Furst, Walker H. Hill, and David R. Krathwohl, eds. 1956. *Taxonomy of Educational Objectives: The Classification of Educational Goals.* New York: David McKay.

Braddock, Richard, Richard Lloyd-Jones, and Lowell Schoer. 1963. *Research in Written Composition.* Urbana, IL: National Council of Teachers of English.

Britton, James, Tony Burgess, Nancy Martin, Alex McLeod, and Harold Rosen. 1975. *The Development of Writing Abilities (11–18).* London: Macmillian.

Calkins, Lucy McCormick. 1983. *Lessons from a Child: On the Teaching and Learning of Writing.* Portsmouth, NH: Heinemann.

———. 1986. *The Art of Teaching Writing.* Portsmouth, NH: Heinemann.

Calkins, Lucy, Shelly Harwayne, and Alex Mitchell. 1987. *The Writing Workshop: A World of Difference* (Videocassette). Portsmouth, NH: Heinemann.

Carroll, Joyce Armstrong and Edward E. Wilson. 1993. *Acts of Teaching: How to Teach Writing.* Englewood, CO: Teacher Ideas Press.

Carroll, Joyce Armstrong. 2002. *Dr. Jac's Guide to Writing with Depth.* Spring, TX: Absey & Co.

———. 2004. *Conclusions: The Unicorns of Composition.* Spring, TX: Absey & Co.

Clay, Marie. 1979. *The Early Detection of Reading Difficulties.* Portsmouth, NH: Heinemann.

Cowan, Gregory, and Elizabeth Cowan. 1980. *Writing.* New York: John Wiley.

Darling-Hammond, L. 2000. "Teacher Quality and Student Achievement: A Review of State Policy Evidence." *Educational Policy Analysis Archives* 8 (1): 1–42.

Edmondson, Jacqueline, and Patrick Shannon. 2002. "The Will of the People." *The Reading Teacher* 55 (February): 452–54.

Eldredge, J. Lloyd, and Dennie Butterfield. 1986. "Alternatives to Traditional Reading Instruction." *The Reading Teacher,* 40 (October): 32–37.

Emig, Janet. 1971. *The Composing Process of Twelfth Graders.* Urbana, IL: National Council of Teachers of English.

Fletcher, Ralph, and JoAnn Portalupi. 1998. *Craft Lessons: Teaching Writing K–8.* Portland, ME: Stenhouse.

Gentry, J. Richard. 1987. *Spel . . . is a Four-Letter Word.* Portsmouth, NH: Heinemann.

Geye, Susan. 1997. *Minilessons for Revision: How to Teaching Writing Skills, Language Usage, Grammar, and Mechanics in the Writing Process.* Spring, TX: Absey & Co.

Gillet, Jean Wallace, and Charles Temple. 1986. *Understanding Reading Problems: Assessment and Instruction.* 2nd ed. Boston, MA: Little, Brown and Co.

Gollasch, Frederick V., ed. 1982. *The Selected Writings of Kenneth S. Goodman Vol. 1: Process, Theory, Research.* Boston: Routledge & Kegan Paul.

Goodman, Kenneth S. 1973. "Miscues: Windows on the Reading Process." In *Miscue Analysis: Applications to Reading Instruction,* ed. Kenneth Goodman. Urbana IL: ERIC Clearinghouse on Reading and Communication Skills and the National Council of Teachers of English.

———. 1996. *Ken Goodman on Reading: A Common Sense Look at the Nature of Language and the Science of Reading.* Portsmouth, NH: Heinemann.

———. 1987. "Beyond Basal Readers: Taking Charge of Your Own Teaching." *Learning* 16 (September): 62–65.

Goodman, Yetta. 1978. "Kidwatching: An Alternative to Testing." *Journal of National Elementary School Principal* 574: 22–27.

Goodman, Yetta. M., Dorothy J. Watson, and Carolyn L. Burke. 2005. *Reading Miscue Inventory: Alternative Procedures.* New York: Richard C. Owen.

———. 1989. "Roots of the Whole-language Movement." *Elementary School Journal* 90 (2): 113–127.

Graves, Donald. 1978. *Balance the Basics: Let Them Write.* New York: Ford Foundation.

———. 1983. *Writing: Teachers and Children at Work.* Portsmouth, NH: Heinemann.

Hansen, Jane. 1987. *When Writers Read.* Portsmouth, NH: Heinemann.

———. 1998. *When Learners Evaluate.* Portsmouth, NH: Heinemann.

Holdaway, Don. 1984. *Stability and Change in Literacy Learning.* Portsmouth, NH: Heinemann.

Hynds, Susan. 1990. "Reading as a Social Event." In *Beyond Communication: Reading Comprehension and Criticism,* ed. Deane Boddan and Stanley B. Straw. Portsmouth, NH: Boynton/Cook.

Kiefer, Barbara, Susan Hepler, and Janet Hickman. 2007. *Charlotte Huck's Children's Literature in the Elementary School.* New York: McGraw Hill.

King, Stephen. 2000. *On Writing: A Memoir of Craft.* New York: Scribner.

Kozol, Jonathan. 1985. *Illiterate America.* New York: Doubleday.

Krashen, Stephen. 2003. *Explorations in Language Acquisition and Use.* Portsmouth, NH: Heinemann.

———. 2004a. "False Claims About Literacy Development." *Educational Leadership* 61 (March): 18.

———. 2004b. *The Power of Reading: Insights from the Research.* 2nd ed. Portsmouth, NH: Heinemann.

Lane, Barry. 1993. *After the End: Teaching and Learning Creative Revision.* Portsmouth, NH: Heinemann.

Manzo, A. V. 1969. "The ReQuest Procedure." *The Journal of Reading* 13 (2): 123–26.

Maslow, Abraham H. 1943. "A Theory of Human Motivation." In *Psychological Review* 50: 372–96.

Morrow, Leslie M. 1992. "The Impact of a Literature-based Program on Literacy Achievement, Use of Literature and Attitudes of Children From Minority Backgrounds." *Reading Research Quarterly* 27 (3): 252–75.

Murray, Donald M. 1979. "Write Before Writing." In *Composition and Its Teaching,* ed. Richard C. Gebhardt. Findlay, OH: Ohio Council of Teachers of English Language Arts.

———. 1985. *A Writer Teaches Writing.* Boston: Houghton Mifflin.

Newman, Judith. 1985. *The Craft of Children's Writing.* Portsmouth, NH: Heinemann.

Norton, Donna E., and Saundra E. Norton. 2007. *Through the Eyes of a Child: An Introduction to Children's Literature.* 7th ed. Upper Saddle River, NJ: Prentice Hall.

Ohanian, Susan. 1999. *One Size Fits Few: The Folly of Educational Standards.* Portsmouth, NH: Heinemann.

Peck, Richard. 1978. "Ten Questions to Ask About a Novel." *The ALAN Review,* (Spring): 17.

Piaget. Jean. 1969. *The Language and Thought of the Child.* New York: Meridian.

Portalupi, JoAnn, and Ralph Fletcher. 2004. *Teaching the Qualities of Writing.* Portsmouth, NH: Heinemann.

Probst, Robert. 1988. "Dialogue with a Text." *The English Journal* 88 (January): 32–38.

Rosenblatt, Louise M. 1978. *The Reader, the Text, the Poem.* Carbondale, IL: Southern Illinois University Press.

———. 1983. *Literature as Exploration.* 4th ed. New York: Modern Language Association of America. (Original work published 1938.)

Smith, Frank. 1985. *Reading Without Nonsense.* New York: Teachers College Press.

———. 1986. *Insult to Intelligence: The Bureaucratic Invasion of American Classrooms.* New York: Arbor House.

———. 1987. *Joining the Literacy Club: Further Essays into Education.* Portsmouth, NH: Heinemann.

———. 2003. *Unspeakable Acts: Unnatural Practices—Flaws and Fallacies in "Scientific" Reading Instruction.* Portsmouth, NH: Heinemann.

Smith, Frank, and Kenneth Goodman. 1971. "On the Psycholinguistic Method of Reading." *Elementary School Journal* 71 (January): 172–81.

Stauffer, Russell G. 1975. *Directing the Reading–Thinking Process.* New York: Harper and Row.

———. 1980. *The Language Experience Approach to the Teaching of Reading.* New York: HarperCollins.

Stillman, Peter R. 1989. *Families Writing.* Cincinnati, OH: Writer's Digest Books.

Taylor, Barbara M., Barbara J. Frye, and Geoffrey M. Maruyama. 1990. "Time spent reading and reading growth." *American Educational Research Journal* 27 (Summer): 351–62.

Vygotsky, Lev. 1962. *Thought and Language.* Ed. Eugenia Haufmann and Gertrude Vakar. Cambridge: Massachusetts Institute of Technology.

Weaver, Connie. 1996a. "On the Teaching of Grammar." Michigan English Language Arts Framework Project. Issued as a SLATE Starter Sheet by the National Council of Teachers of English. In *Creating Support for Effective Literacy Education,* C. Weaver, L. Gillmeister-Krause, and G. Vento-Zogby. Portsmouth, NH: Heinemann.

———. 1996b. "On the Teaching of Skills in Context." Michigan English Language Arts Framework project. Issued as a SLATE Starter Sheet by the National Council of Teachers of English. In *Creating Support for Effective Literacy Education,* C. Weaver, L. Gillmeister-Krause, and G. Vento-Zogby. Portsmouth, NH: Heinemann.

———. 1996c. "On the Teaching of Spelling." Michigan English Language Arts Framework Project. Issued as a SLATE Starter Sheet by the National Council of Teachers of English. In *Creating Support for Effective Literacy Education,* C. Weaver, L. Gillmeister-Krause, and G. Vento-Zogby. Portsmouth, NH: Heinemann.

Children's and Young Adult Books

Avi. 1996. *Wolf Rider.* New York: Simon & Schuster.

Baylor, Byrd. 1986. *I'm in Charge of Celebrations.* New York: Macmillan.

Bertrand, Diane. 1999. *Trino's Choice.* New York: Piñata Books.

Bulla, Dale. 1995. *My Brother's a Pain in the Backseat.* Austin, TX: New Horizon Educational Services Press.

Cooney, Caroline B. 1990. *The Face on the Milk Carton.* New York: Bantam Doubleday Dell.

Crews, Donald. 1991. *Bigmama's.* New York: Greenwillow Books.

Curtis, Christopher Paul. 1993. *The Watsons Go to Birmingham—1963.* New York: Random House.

———. 1999. *Bud, Not Buddy.* New York: Random House.

DiCamillo, Kate. 2000. *Because of Winn-Dixie.* New York: Scholastic.

———. 2002. *The Tiger Rising.* New York: Candlewick.

Duncan, Lois 1973. *I Know What You Did Last Summer.* New York: Bantam Doubleday Dell.

———. 1976. *Summer of Fear.* New York: Dell Laurel-Leaf.

———. 1978. *Killing Mr. Griffin.* New York: Bantam Doubleday Dell.

———. 1989. *Don't Look Behind You.* New York: Bantam Doubleday Dell.

———. 1992. *Who Killed My Daughter?* New York: Dell.

Fox, Mem. 1984. *Wilfred Gordon McDonald Partridge.* La Jolla, CA: Kane Miller.

Gantos, Jack. 2001. *Joey Pigza Swallowed the Key.* New York: Learning Links, Inc.

Griffiths, Andy. 2001. *The Day My Butt Went Psycho!* New York: Scholastic.

Haddix, Margaret Peterson. 1998. *Among the Hidden.* New York: Aladdin.

Haynes, Betsy. *The Fabulous Five.* New York: Skylark.

Holman, Felice. 1974. *Slake's Limbo.* New York: Scribner.

Holt, Kimberly Willis. 1999. *When Zachary Beaver Comes to Town*. New York: Henry Holt and Company.

Kehret, Peg. 2005. *The Ghost's Grave*. New York: Scholastic.

Klass, David. 2001. *You Don't Know Me*. New York: HarperCollins.

Korman, Gordon. 2002. *No More Dead Dogs*. New York: Hyperion.

Little, Bentley. 2000. *The Walking*. New York: Signet.

MacLachlan, Patricia. 1994. *All the Places to Love*. New York: HarperCollins.

MacLachlan, Patrica. 2004. *Baby*. New York: Yearling.

Martin Jr., Bill. 1988. *Ghost Eye Tree*. New York: Henry Holt and Company.

McLerran, Alice. 1981. *Roxaboxen*. Boston: Lothrop.

Myers, Walter Dean. 1999. *Monster*. New York: Scholastic.

Nixon, Joan Lowery. 1986. *The Other Side of Dark*. New York: Dell Laurel-Leaf.

———. 1989. *Whispers from the Dead*. New York: Dell Laurel-Leaf.

———. 1993. *The Name of the Game Was Murder*. New York: Bantam Doubleday Dell.

———. 1995. *If You Were a Writer*. New York: Simon & Schuster.

Philbrick, Rodman. 2001. *Freak the Mighty*. New York: Scholastic.

Rowling, J. K. 2001. *Harry Potter and the Sorcerer's Stone*. New York: Scholastic.

Rylant, Cynthia. 1985. *When the Relatives Came*. New York: Bradbury Press.

Sachar, Louis. 1998. *Holes*. New York: Scholastic.

Snicket, Lemony. 1999. *A Series of Unfortunate Events: The Bad Beginning*. New York: HarperCollins.

Soto, Gary. 1994. *Too Many Tamales*. New York: Scholastic.

Spinelli, Jerry. 2000. *Stargirl*. New York: Random House.

———. 2002. *Maniac Magee*. New York: Scholastic.

Stine, R. L. 1990. *The Boyfriend*. New York: Scholastic.

Strasser, Todd. 1999. *Give a Boy a Gun*. New York: Simon & Schuster.

Van Draanen, Wendelin. 2006. *Runaway*. New York: Random House.

Voigt, Cynthia. 1986. *Izzy, Willy-Nilly*. New York: Simon & Schuster.

Waber, Bernard. 1972. *Ira Sleeps Over*. New York: Houghton Mifflin.

Acknowledgments

In 1983 I walked into the superintendent's office in a small rural school in Lovelady, Texas to apply to substitute teach and walked out as the junior high remedial reading teacher. With degrees in business and English, I knew nothing about teaching reading. That job challenged me more than anything in my life to that point. It challenged me with questions I had no answers for.

In the summer of 1985, after promptings from my mentor, friend, and colleague, Jackie Gerla, I attended the New Jersey Writing Project in Texas at Sam Houston State University. It was there that I met Joyce Armstrong Carroll and Eddie Wilson. Joyce and Eddie's obvious passion for reading, writing, and learning ignited that same spark in me. I became a writer and a learner that summer and was introduced to the work of Janet Emig, Donald Murray, Donald Graves, Peter Elbow, Lucy Calkins, and other great theorists and researchers. Thanks to Joyce, Eddie, Judy Bramlett, and Bess Osburn for making that life-changing experience possible. That summer writing institute laid the foundation for the rest of my teaching career.

Eager to learn more, I returned to the university the next summer for my first reading course. Based on the assessment training I received from Sheila Cohen and my case study student Dexter, I knew that I could not go back to the classroom and put all my students in the same basal reader. Again searching for answers, my quest led me to Joan Prouty who introduced me to the work of Don Holdaway and the independent reading program. Joan mentored me through my first year of workshop teaching. The next summer, Bess Osburn introduced me to the work of Louise Rosenblatt, Marie Clay, Frank Smith, and Yetta and Ken Goodman, the cueing systems and the miscue analysis. Through miscue training and my case study with Susan, I learned the power of listening to readers and using assessment to inform instruction. My learning continued through my master's classes, through my training process to become a NJWPT trainer, and through books like Nancie Atwell's *In the Middle* and Jane Hansen's *When Writers Read*. These experiences inspired, motivated, and invigorated me and kept me going through challenging times.

Without the support of administrators, my dream could not have become a reality. Mr. Crowe provided me with grant money to set up a classroom library, freed me to teach kids and not curriculum, and allowed me to manipulate the schedule in order to have my students for a two-period block for reading and writing. He and other administrators after him allowed me to grow as a teacher. And, of course, I learned most from my students who first challenged me with questions like, "When are we going to do some work?" or "When are you going to teach us something?" but settled into the workshop, allowing me to learn with them as we observed their growth as readers and writers.

Thanks to John Stansell and Leslie Patterson for encouraging me to pursue a doctorate. Through my mentors at Texas A&M University—John Stansell, Donna Wiseman, Joyce Many, Ernie Stringer, and others—I learned about teacher change and professional development models. The work of John Goodlad, the Holmes Group, and Sid Richardson Foundation informed my later work with teachers in school/university partnerships. Ernie Stringer and his community-based action research model and the work of Michael Fullan, Bruce Joyce, Beverly Showers, and others provided me with a framework for working with teachers in numerous long-term professional development opportunities.

Thanks to Elvia Rodriguez who supported me in my early years of university teaching at Stephen F. Austin State University, allowing me to open three field-based reading-writing workshop research sites. She always trusted me and freed me to spread my wings. This freedom invigorated me and allowed me to see that workshop works anywhere, in any setting. Sandra Sherman, the best school administrator I've ever known, invited me into schools in the university area, making my dream a reality. A special thank you to the principals and teachers there and in districts around the state who invited me into their schools and their classrooms to assist them in implementing workshop. I must also thank my friend and colleague, Sharon Lewis, who has supported me through the years and responded to early drafts of this book even before the first draft became a written reality.

Thanks to my mom, my first teacher, who taught me through her example to work hard and to persevere in the face of adversity, to James who supported me financially and emotionally through three degrees and through those early years as a struggling teacher, and to my children who have taught me more about teaching, learning, loving, and life than I could ever have imagined possible. Brian taught me what can happen when kids are given early opportunities to read and write. Dana taught me to have compassion for struggling readers. Through her struggles and eventual successes, she inspired me with a passionate desire to not let any child fall through the cracks. Through my work with Jamie in various capacities, first as her middle school teacher, then college professor, program director, and now co-author of this book, I have been inspired and supported. Jennifer, now a fabulous workshop teacher, trusted Jamie and me to mentor her through her first year of teaching, an experience that reminded us once again of the magical power of the workshop classroom.

Linda Ellis
The Woodlands, TX
June 1, 2007

M y mother ends her acknowledgments by thanking her family, and I must certainly begin mine by thanking her. In doing so it is my intention to thank all of those who inspired her.

My mother is my greatest mentor. I am eternally grateful to her for instilling in me at a very young age a love of reading and writing. She is a true example of what it means to be a lifelong learner. I admire her endless search for knowledge and commend her passion and desire to be a better teacher, to continue learning in order to help her children and her students become even more successful, lifelong readers and writers.

I lived the reading and writing workshop for the first time in her sixth grade language arts classroom. It was in the corners of this classroom, tucked away with my favorite series' books and writing folder in hand, where I first envisioned being a real author one day. I remember the overwhelming joy I felt when I brought my very own published book to our first author's day. It was in her classroom where I truly learned to love reading and writing. I thank her for this experience.

My mother's dedication to teaching and learning has had a lasting impact on me as a student and a teacher. I wouldn't be the teacher I am today without her showing me the way. Having experienced reading and writing workshop as a student, seeing first-hand the impact it had on my life, I knew I had to share this experience with others. I knew I must keep this kind of teaching and learning alive in schools. I wanted to become a workshop teacher so I could help others gain a love of reading and writing.

When I made the decision to become a teacher, my mother was there. I was fortunate to have her as a college reading professor where she introduced me to her mentors, teaching me what they had taught her. I devoured Nancie Atwell's *In the Middle* and Carol Avery's *...And With a Light Touch*. Their stories helped my perspective of reading and writing workshop transition from that of the student to that of the teacher, and they showed me how to implement workshop with my own students. I was forever changed by their powerful books and am grateful to them for sharing their stories.

I must also thank the mentor teachers who opened up their classrooms to me during this time of transition and learning as a preservice teacher. Jana McCall and Jill Hines showed me what a reading and writing workshop classroom looks like in a first- and second-grade multiage classroom. I will never forget their phenomenal writing minilessons and the remarkable growth their students made as readers and writers that year. Judy Northrup trusted me, as her student teacher, to be her teaching partner, helping her implement reading workshop for the first time with six classes of sixth grade students. I learned so much from her that semester about classroom management and the importance of having a strong support network—even if it's just one other person on campus to dialogue with. We stood by each other as colleagues and friends, moving to a new school the following year and going against the grain yet again to implement reading and writing workshop with our middle school students.

I must also thank my first principal, Karen Archer, and assistant principal, Karen Liska, for believing in me as a first year teacher and trusting me to do what I knew was best for my students. I have been blessed with supportive administrators who have given me the professional freedom to develop workshops with my students. They, along with Sharon Lewis, Bill Lakin, Laurie

Ballering, and Dan Hacking, have shown me just how critical administrative support is, especially in our current high-stakes, test-driven environment. I admire the administrators who stand up for their teachers and allow best practices to prevail in the classroom, acting as buffers against the outside pressure to fill our days with mindless stuff.

I must also thank Joyce Armstrong Carroll and Eddie Wilson for the New Jersey Writing Project in Texas. It was during this three-week summer writing institute that I reconnected with myself as a writer. After years of high school English courses that slowly drained the passion for reading and writing out of me, this summer institute rekindled my passion. It made me the writing teacher I am because it made me a writer again. I thank them for sharing their knowledge and expertise with me in the institute, in the books they have written, and in their annual conferences, retreats, and workshops I have attended.

I have also found mentors in the authors of the professional books I have read. Donald Graves, Donald Murray, Frank Smith, Ken and Yetta Goodman, Richard Allington, Jane Hansen, Linda Rief, Lucy Calkins, Jim Trelease, Ralph Fletcher, JoAnn Portalupi, and Barry Lane acted as cheerleaders and supported me from the pages of their books. Their research and publications continue to empower me to do what is right for my students despite the political climate I work in. The more I read, the more I want to learn and the more I realize there is to learn. I will always be in the process of learning because these mentors have instilled in me a passion to learn.

Great friends have also supported my journey of learning. I would like to thank my colleague and friend, Katie Ross. Her genuine friendship helped carry me from one deadline to another as she eagerly listened to my writing, thoughts, and ideas and offered her wise feedback and encouragement. I would also like to thank my dear friend, Bryant Pettey, who has supported my journey for many years, always encouraging me to be honest with myself and to take risks that will push me towards even greater things in life. He has taught me what it means to be an unconditional friend.

And my acknowledgments wouldn't be complete without thanking my father, James Ellis, for always supporting me—no matter what path I choose to pursue. He taught me that I could achieve whatever I put my mind to. His encouraging words, "Go for it!" ring in my ears every time I take a chance.

I especially want to thank my best friend and greatest supporter, my husband Robert Marsh. He believes in me, loves me, and is proud of me. I am in awe of his knowledge and creativity. He is the most talented writer I know. Every time he edits my work and offers feedback, I learn something new about writing. He teaches and inspires me daily. His passion for reading and writing, his endless creative ideas, and his strong desire to continue learning and pursuing his dreams makes him the most amazing person I know.

Last, but certainly not least, I must thank all of my intermediate and middle-school students who read, wrote, and shared their lives with me daily. They taught me how to be a better reader, writer, listener, thinker, and teacher. I am thankful that they have allowed me to share our stories and journeys of growth and learning with others. This book would not be possible without them. Their voices reside in its pages.

Jamie Marsh
Charlottesville, VA
June 1, 2007

Together, we would like to thank all those at Heinemann who made this book possible. Our first thanks goes to Lois Bridges for having faith in our work and being our cheerleader. She always knew just the right words to inspire us and to make us want to write. Lois was quick to respond to early drafts with encouragement and helpful suggestions. We will be forever grateful because we know she made this book possible. Lisa Luedeke's editorial skills and her careful first edits and prompt responses to our questions moved the manuscript forward to production. Thanks to all the others at Heinemann who worked behind the scenes: Leigh Peake, Alan Huisman, Stephanie Colado, Doria Turner, Sonja Chapman, Kim Arney, and Eric Chalek. This has truly been a learning process, and the entire Heinemann team has helped us along the way.

Linda Ellis
Jamie Marsh

Index